THE
SECRET WORLD OF THE
FREEMASONS

THIS IS A CARLTON BOOK

Text and design copyright © 2009
Carlton Books Limited

First published in 2006.

This edition published in 2009 by
Carlton Books Limited
20 Mortimer Street
London W1T 3JW

10 9 8 7 6 5 4 3 2

A CIP catalogue record for this book is available
from the British Library.

ISBN 978 1 84732 479 5

Printed and bound in Dubai

Executive Editor: Lisa Dyer
Art Editor: Emma Wicks
Design: Simon Wilder
Copy Editor: Jonathan Hilton
Picture Editor: Sarah Edwards
Production: Caroline Alberti

THE SECRET WORLD OF THE FREEMASONS

TIM DEDOPULOS

CARLTON
BOOKS

CONTENTS

Introduction

What is Freemasonry?

Rumours and legends have dogged Freemasonry since its inception. Everyone you talk to seems to have a different take. It's a secret conspiracy of power that rules the world. No, it's the inheritor of the wealth and mysteries of the Knights Templar … a club to give harmless old men something to do during the week … a Satanic conspiracy to destroy mankind for ever … a huge, corrupt, old-boys' network … the guardian of great occult secrets … a blasphemous religion … one big charity fund-raising group. There are a thousand theories, but the truth is something altogether stranger and more wondrous.

The official traditional answer – the one you will probably get if you go and ask a Grand Lodge about the Craft – is that Freemasonry is "a peculiar system of morality, veiled in allegory and illuminated by symbols". There's no denying that the answer sounds evocative, but what does it mean and, more importantly, what does it quietly imply?

Lodge Masters past and present celebrate the 275th anniversary of the founding of the United Grand Lodge of England at Earl's Court, London, 1992.

This symbol-packed engraving pays honour to Freemasonry's charitable spirit and good works.

At its simplest level, Freemasonry is one of the world's oldest surviving secular fraternal societies. Although it is specifically not religious, its members are concerned with developing themselves morally and spiritually in order to become better people. Over the course of their time as members, they are taught the society's principles through a series of ritual dramas, rather like prewritten plays. These make use of ancient words, actions and settings, and are explained through allegorical reference to the trappings of the stonemasons' craft, particularly its tools and customs.

The single most critical qualification required to become a Freemason is that you have to believe in God or some other supreme deity. It doesn't matter what religion you follow, or how dedicated you are to it. All belief systems are welcome, even the home-brewed ones, and how strictly you follow your religion's dictates is left entirely up to your own conscience. The important thing is that you have faith in a supreme being. The reason should be obvious – if you don't believe that there is a spiritual side to life, you can't genuinely claim to be interested in your spiritual development, and so the whole thing would be a bit pointless for you.

Apart from that, what you believe absolutely doesn't matter. Freemasonry never pries into a member's religion – in fact, all religious discussion is utterly forbidden during Masonic meetings, as is any political debate. Such matters are deeply held personal issues and are likely to prove divisive. In an organization that seeks members of good repute from all races, religions and creeds, avoiding political and religious clashes is vital.

Pythagoras (left) and a musician (right) represent the nobility of the liberal arts in this medieval image. The pursuit of knowledge and interest in science and the arts touch at the core of the Freemason's journey toward self-improvement.

There is, of course, far more to Freemasonry than just a series of moral and spiritual teachings. There is a number of other "sides" to it that arise from its core purpose. One of the most important of these is that Freemasonry is a very charitable organization. For 1994, it is estimated that the collected Grand Lodges and their constituent members across the USA donated a sum of $625 million to national and local charitable causes alone, with perhaps as much as an additional $400 million going to international funds. But this is just the tip of the iceberg, as a great many Masons volunteer their time. The Masonic Service Association, for example, ensures that every Veteran's Administration Hospital in America has a Masonic volunteer working with patients

– half a million hours' worth of work a year. By comparison, in Detroit as many as a thousand local Masons regularly turn out as part of the efforts to help patrol the city on "Devil's Night", October 30, to try to prevent the annual epidemic of fires and looting associated with that night. Their efforts have kept their assigned territory of the city entirely clear of damage for several years.

In Britain, the Craft's members contribute more than £3 million annually to national and international – non-Masonic – charitable causes, ranging from the hospice movement and the Prince's Trust to Alzheimer's research and housing for disadvantaged inner-city children. In addition, each lodge contributes toward local non-Masonic charities. Amounts vary, but the total given to local charities is typically around £100,000 per year for a county with a reasonable Masonic presence. In Australia and New Zealand, charitable activities are similarly distributed across different levels of the organization. Regional United Grand Lodges have their own programmes that operate in addition to a variety of charitable organizations and to the efforts of individual normal lodges (known as Symbolic or Craft Lodges). Even so, the total efforts across the two countries are thought to raise more than AU$6 million annually.

Another important aspect of Freemasonry is that it is a social experience. All Freemasons know in advance that they share certain attitudes and expectations in common, and that provides a good base for getting to know one another. To be accepted as an initiate, an existing Freemason has to vouch for you as a decent, socially responsible person, and you then have to convince the majority of the lodge of the same. Every other Mason will have had to pass similar examination. As a member, you know that the people you will meet are interested in learning and improving themselves as human beings, and that you will have had similar experiences in lodge ritual. That all comes together to provide a strong basis for friendship, even before you take into account the social aspects of the meetings.

As previously mentioned, Freemasonry is also educational. Its entire structure is geared around teaching and illuminating through the symbolic and allegorical content of the lodges and the ritual that takes place inside them. The Craft is founded on the basis that its members should all seek to gain greater knowledge of the universe and their role within it. Even outside of its own teachings, members are encouraged to learn as much as possible about the arts and sciences. This is quite apart from the work of spiritual and moral philosophy that the Craft seeks to teach through its rituals. Over the centuries it has sought to agree on fundamental truths that all right-minded people can agree on, regardless of political or religious affiliation; these are the foundations of the rituals that form the focus of group meetings.

These are some of the more important elements that go into making the whole experience of Masonry. However, it is also worth considering some of the things

that it does not include. Above all, Freemasonry is very specifically not a religion. It does have certain quasi-religious trappings, and that can make it look religious if you don't look too clearly. Particularly, the requirement to believe in a supreme being – and the reliance on allegorical rituals as a teaching device – suggests religious leanings. Morality and spiritual development are a strong basis for developing religious interests, after all. However, this is nothing more than a surface gloss.

Freemasonry does not claim to offer a route to salvation or a means to contact God. It does not have any solutions for the world's ills, other than to try to be decent, upstanding people. It does not claim any understanding of evil – or of good, for that matter. It has no answers for sorrow, or grief, and claims no knowledge of what happens when you die. It does not know anything of the punishments for transgression. It has no dogma whatsoever. All religions, by definition, must offer some way of mediating and explaining the spiritual world and its requirements. Masonry merely tries to help its members to become better people.

This is not always clear to external viewpoints. Some decades ago, the Catholic Church reversed its prior position and declared that no Catholic was allowed to be a member of the Freemasons. Not all Catholics have followed this ban, of course; the Craft itself bars no faith. Any who seek membership are welcome. The reasons for the prohibition are still murky; certainly there seems to be nothing in Masonic ritual or tradition that disagrees with Roman Catholic teachings.

Freemasonry is also very much not a political organization. All discussion of political issues is expressly forbidden at Masonic meetings. Political beliefs are some of the most deeply held, personal and divisive elements of any person's character, and if Freemasonry attempted to take a political stance, it would split itself into a myriad of fragments. With no possibility of political debate, it cannot have a political direction or ulterior motive. Even the possibility of Masonry being hijacked for some covert political purpose is blocked, in fact.

Despite the wild rantings of the occasional Internet loon, Freemasonry is not a single, united body. In fact, it is about as far from being a coherent entity as it is possible for one movement to be. Each Grand Lodge

A new Catholic priest is ordained by Cardinal Bernard Law as the Holy Spirit is passed into him via the laying on of hands in the Roman Catholic rite.

is its own supreme authority. No Grand Lodge or United Grand Lodge has any influence over any other. There is no ranking system or precedence. The officers of a given Grand Lodge are the sole authority over Freemasonry in their territory. Each of the American states, each nation of the United Kingdom, each Australian territory, each country or subdivision is its own Masonic world.

We'll look in a little while at how this structure hangs together with the assistance of a set of common standards and agreed rituals – so that a Mason from one Grand Lodge has the same experience and education as a Mason from another – but no two Grand Lodges see everything in quite the same way. To suggest that this pack of collective fiefdoms could ever unite under one covert political purpose is a grand feat of the imagination.

Another important distinction is that Freemasonry is not a club. While it has some very sociable aspects, its primary purpose is not as a social outlet. Membership of the Freemasons does not come with comprehensive fringe benefits. There's no "members-only lounge bar" offering heavily subsidized cigars and fine brandies. The most common charge laid against Masons is that of nepotism and cronyism, but in fact the society's oaths and obligations specifically forbid members from using the organization in this way. Freemasonry demands that its members respect and honour both the spirit and letter of the law of the country in which they live and work. Not only do its principles not conflict with its members' duties as citizens, they actively attempt to strengthen them by encouraging all Masons to fulfil their personal responsibilities, both in private and in public.

Using membership to promote your own (or anyone else's) interests – financial, professional or personal – is strictly condemned, and is grounds for being thrown out. Members are required not to betray confidences – but only if they are socially acceptable. A Mason's duty as a member of society is explicitly set above any obligation to any other Freemason. Any attempt to protect a Freemason who has broken the law or acted dishonourably is specifically forbidden. Members' interests never come in front of the interests of society in Masonic requirements.

In fact, the structure of Freemasonry doesn't even attempt to provide easy or plentiful chances for networking. Most meetings are taken up with lodge business and ritual, and provide little chance for chit-chat. Even the meal afterward frequently involves semi-ritualized behaviour. Social opportunities exist, of course, but they're not the main order of business. Furthermore, while most members do end up meeting at least a few Masons from other lodges, it is not guaranteed or automatic. There is nothing in the formal practices of Masonry that requires different lodges to come together regularly. It would be perfectly possible – if very unusual – for a member to spend decades within Freemasonry and only ever meet up with fellow lodge members.

None of this is to deny that Masonry is a social experience, as mentioned earlier. The great majority of Masons make plenty of new, good friends over the course

The biblical rebuilding of
Jerusalem after its sacking,
as depicted in Nehemiah,
Chapter 3.

of their Masonic lives. It is one of the great pleasures of being part of the organization. The point, however, is that it is most certainly not Freemasonry's main aim.

Finally, a point that may surprise some readers is that Freemasonry is not a secret society. If it were, it would keep its existence secret. On the contrary, it goes out of its way to make itself as accessible as possible. You'll find local lodges listed in most telephone directories, and certainly most of the Grand Lodges and United Grand Lodges have a very heavy presence on the web, complete with contact numbers. That's hardly very secret.

Membership isn't even secret – while it's usually left to any given Mason to confirm membership, most are proud of the organization and will cheerfully tell anyone of their involvement. There's no central members' register of freemasons worldwide, but then, as mentioned above, there's no central anything. In some areas, there is even a tradition of the local lodge holding a members' parade once or twice a year. Attitudes have wavered over the years, but nowadays just about the only things that the organization asks members to keep strictly confidential are the ways by which one member can recognize another – and those are plastered all over the Internet anyway.

When all is said and done, though, you cannot define something by listing everything that it is not – any more than you can truly understand it by looking at its side-effects. Going back to the very first answer – that it is a system of morality veiled in allegory – we are left with an impression of serious purpose, but little in the way of solid meat. The system offers a selection of truths, both philosophical and scientific, based around the accepted principle that there is one all-mighty, infinite and perfect deity. From this, the intended perfection and completeness of the universe can be inferred, as can its internal correspondences. By working with a general scheme that corresponds to different stages in human and universal existence and a series of lessons embodying these truths, greater moral and social virtue can be achieved. This is wrapped up within the purity of mathematical geometry, and the physical craft that embodies those geometric principles – that of architecture and construction. But even this is merely a statement of the Craft's beliefs and purposes.

So what actually is Freemasonry? You could say that it is a word that summarizes the beliefs and practices of Freemasons worldwide, and the way in which their groups are linked and administered. This is a bit self-defining – Freemasonry is what Freemasons do, basically – but it is at least inclusive. A bit more usefully, this definition could be seen to show Freemasonry as a craft, a personal vocation of benevolent moral growth, whose principles are conveyed through imagery linked to building. According to the German handbook, it is "an activity of closely united men who […] work for the welfare of mankind, striving morally to ennoble themselves and others and thereby bring about a universal league of mankind". Finally, this is approaching accuracy.

Certainly, there must be something compelling about Freemasonry for it to have survived and flourished for three centuries or more. Without some purpose, some aspiration, it would have fallen into oblivion long ago, as so many other organizations have done. Its mission is to help bring the plans of the divine into being. Just as the central symbol of Freemasonry is the construction of the renowned Temple of Solomon in Jerusalem – the very home of God on Earth, the holy of holies – so its central aspiration is the construction of a metaphorical perfect temple of united humanity in peace.

That, at last, brings us to the answer. Freemasonry is a path, clothed in the trappings of the ancient stonemason's craft, blind to faith, ethnicity and social standing, that leads toward morality, humanity and love. The benefits and good works that grow out of it are almost incidental, by-products of striving toward better things. It is a cooperative effort to improve the world, by taking responsibility for yourself and the world around you, and working alongside like-minded people to make things a little better.

The ultimate truth, strange and wondrous as it is, is that Freemasonry is not a religious order, or a secret society, or even really an organization at all. It is a glittering journey – one that leads, optimistically and circuitously, to a better world for all of us.

1

Exoteric Freemasonry

The common image of Freemasonry is that it is one great big entity, a unified whole that reaches across continents. Along with the general misunderstanding that it is a secret society, this imagined structure makes conspiracy-minded people rather nervous, and understandably so. The idea of a huge, sinister, octopus-like secret order peering out across the world from one gigantic, pyramid-framed eye is powerful, seductive, frightening and – fortunately – simply not true.

The reality is that the Masonic world is so varied, territorial and divided that it is almost impossible to talk about "Freemasonry" in general. Like most philosophical and religious systems, Freemasonry has been interpreted and expressed in different ways at various times throughout history. No two Masons have quite the same definition of the Craft; in some cases, their ideas can be radically different. There is no rule or founding principle that hasn't had an exception somewhere or other. The only aspect that every Mason agrees on, in fact, is the importance of Freemasonry itself. Nevertheless, there is a core to the Masonic experience. Most Masons agree on the majority of points. As this chapter shows, the variations and differences simply add extra layers of beauty and interest to the whole.

A Masonic hall in Yeovil, England, serving the town itself and the surrounding area. The glasswork above the door openly announces the building's purpose.

The Internal Structure

Most newcomers to Freemasonry are surprised to discover how chaotic the international structure of the Craft really is. Far from being the frightening, united conspiracy that so many theorists believe, it is instead a highly divided calling – one that cannot truly be thought of as a single organization at all.

At the simplest levels, the structure is fairly straightforward. The core keystone of the Masonic world is the Grand Lodge (alternatively, some are called Grand Orients). This serves an administrative function, bringing together four or more "Symbolic" (regular) lodges and providing them with a common set of rules and regulations. In most cases, the members of a Grand Lodge have formerly served as Master of one or more of its constituent lodges. These Past Masters tend to have no specific duties in their home lodge, and the ones who serve at Grand Lodge possess enough spare time to donate themselves to helping with central administration and other clerical services as required. It is expected that their years of experience in the regular lodges will give them enough insight to be in a good position to help steer the group.

The Grand Lodge

The key attribute that every Grand Lodge has in common, in theory, is its adherence to the "Landmarks" of Freemasonry – the guiding principles that make up the very heart and core of the Craft. Unfortunately, there tend to be as many different opinions as to what the Landmarks actually are as there are Freemasons. Noting the potentially divisive nature of the issue, some Grand Lodges specifically do not attempt to define the Landmarks at all (although, informally, they have a pretty close idea). So, in reality, the only absolutely common ground is that each Grand Lodge agrees that there are Landmarks that define the Craft.

For the most part, Grand Lodges tend to be organized territorially. In countries with a relatively light Masonic presence or a comparatively compact landmass, there may be a single Grand Lodge that serves the entire nation. If the country's lodges are numerous enough and distant from each other, however, then the country may be divided up into regions, with each territory or state having its own Grand Lodge.

It is not always that simple, of course. In many cases, historical events leave Grand Lodges with territories that may overlap, even within the same strand of Masonry. However, each Symbolic Lodge is attached to – and follows – just one Grand Lodge, so even in an area in which two or more Grand Lodges hold sway, any given Freemason will be under no confusion as to which body he is linked.

In addition to the basic structure above, some regions are large enough that the Grand Lodge cannot easily represent all of its membership. In these instances, a middle layer of Provincial (or District) Grand Lodges is put in place. These, as the name suggests, are junior offshoots of the Grand Lodge responsible for a part – a province – of the Grand Lodge's territory. Where a Provincial Grand Lodge is in place, a local lodge will typically deal with its Provincial Grand Lodge, and the Provincial Grand Lodges will take business on to the Grand Lodge proper. To muddy the water further, some Grand Lodges are referred to as "United". This is most commonly the case when two or more competing regional Grand Lodges have put aside their differences and merged back into one single body, but it can also indicate that a Grand Lodge has made use of a network of Provincial Grand Lodges beneath it.

Each Grand Lodge is its own sovereign power. It is as simple as that. There is no higher body or structure; once a Grand Lodge has been formed, it is free to do as it wills. In practice, of course, that means that it follows the general needs of its lodges, because there are always opportunities for a lodge to break away from one Grand Lodge and attach itself to a different one – or to gather some other groups and form a new one. However, setting aside the membership's right to vote with its feet, a Grand Lodge is answerable to nobody. It can choose to modify which forms of the standard ritual its lodges may perform, it can set membership policies, raise or lower dues, alter the structure of lodge meetings, and generally tinker as it sees fit. Most, of course, stick with the rules and regulations that they inherited from their founder lodges.

In addition to directing general policy with regards to the specifics of the way Freemasonry is practised by its lodges, a Grand Lodge also takes care of a number of other

The United Grand Lodge of England meets with all the pomp and splendour expected of the world's oldest Grand Lodge. Here, the Duke of Kent, the Grand Master, greets fellow Masons to mark the lodge's 275th anniversary.

central functions. Each lodge donates a certain amount of money a year to the Grand Lodge in the form of assorted dues and fees toward equipment, tokens of initiation and so on. That money is budgeted at the Grand Lodge's annual general meeting by a members' vote, and typically goes toward paying any full-time central administrative staff (reception staff, security and so on) or professionals (lawyers and accountants, for example) as may be needed, maintaining such properties, museums and other projects as may be on the books, organizing occasional all-member social events, preparing member newsletters and similar activities. The greatest single budget item, however, is almost invariably the collected charitable causes.

Following on from the dictates that charity begins at home – in other words, locally – each lodge supports charities in its home area. For most lodges, that means paying into causes to improve the town or city district

This colour lithograph of the French School depicts the beliefs and duties of Freemasons attached to the eighteenth-century Grand Orient d'France.

that they are based in. Other lodges with a non-geographic basis – veterans' lodges, for example – support causes based around their own particular interests. That leaves the Grand Lodge to provide money for assorted regional and national causes. The sorts of sums donated have already been discussed, and tend to be fairly impressive. Many Grand Lodges also administer and fund internal charities to help support Masons' elderly widows and orphans and to provide some emergency relief to members in severe financial trouble. These internal charities tend to be quite limited in scope, however, as one of the most universally accepted of the Craft's Landmarks is that Freemasonry should not be a source of or route to material benefit for its members.

Recognition and Regulation of Lodges

Another fact not commonly realized outside the Craft itself is that Freemasonry comes in quite a wide variety of different "flavours". The rites and rituals of initiation and teaching have frequently been modified over the centuries as various philosophical and spiritual ideas gained and lost popularity, and there is now a wide range of different styles of basic Masonry. Although most of the common forms remain broadly similar, some variants are actually profoundly different. Each Grand Lodge decides for itself which variants it considers "real" Freemasonry, and which variants are too far removed to remain true. The same, of course, goes for the greater issues of how (and indeed whether) to define the Landmarks, what criteria are required for member Masons, and so on. Although the general structure remains the same, the particulars can become quite widely disparate.

This all leads directly to the thorny and often confusing issue of "recognition". In order to make sure that Masons were not put in vulnerable positions or left at risk of being conned, early Masonic groups agreed that their members would be allowed to take part in another lodge's meetings only if the other lodge was recognized as "Regular". That way, the Grand Lodges could ensure that their members weren't going to get sucked into some quasi-Masonic cult. The principle of recognition was quickly adopted as a Landmark.

However, whether or not any given lodge is judged regular or not is, like everything else regarding Masonry, at the sole discretion of each Grand Lodge. There is a set of criteria used to judge regularity, including adherence to the Landmarks, the precise minutiae of the lodge's original creation, membership requirements and dues, benefits of membership and so on. Naturally, no two Grand Lodges have exactly the same set of criteria.

The issue does have some notable ramifications. A Freemason is, as you would expect, allowed to fraternize – associate as a Mason – with any other Mason associated with the same Grand Lodge. In order to preserve Masonry's ideals of fellowship, members are also allowed to fraternize with members associated with any other regular Grand Lodge. Although there may be some differences in ritual, it is accepted that a Master Mason can take part in all the lodge proceedings of any regular lodge – with an invitation, anyway. However, it is a serious breach of protocol to take part in any Masonic meeting of a lodge that has been judged irregular – it will usually result in the member's expulsion for misconduct.

While it's very unlikely that you would get into trouble visiting other lodges in your local area, the international field is an entirely different matter. In any foreign area, Masons are always strongly encouraged to make sure that they have established whether or not the local Grand Lodge is considered regular back home.

There is no easy way to guess regarding matters of regularity. There is no common ground. Certifying regularity normally takes an extensive investigation into the Grand Lodge in question – one that each other Grand Lodge has to undertake in its own time and at its own expense. In some cases, questions about the status of just one individual local lodge may be enough to result in an entire Grand Lodge being ruled irregular. It depends on the investigators. Certain forms of ritual may be acceptable to some Grand Lodges, but not to others; the same goes for admissions policies or historical precedents, or the issue might be decided for reasons of political expedience. There is no requirement (or even

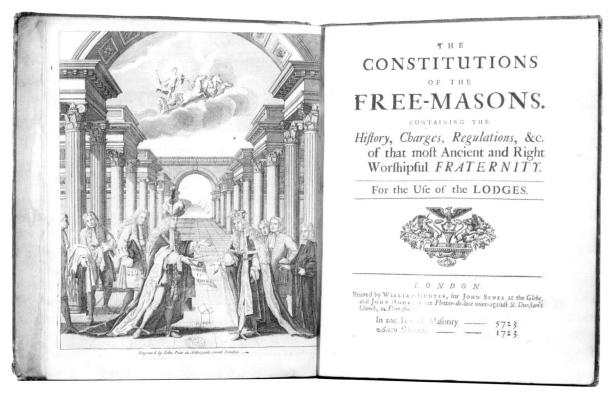

Dr James Anderson's Masonic constitution was published in 1723 in London, and provided a united shape and form that Freemasonry has followed ever since.

specific trend) automatically to recognize a Grand Lodge that recognizes you.

Historical issues can further cloud matters. In a few cases, old slights and rivalries may be carried through as a refusal to grant recognition. The opposite can happen, too, of course; a Grand Lodge may feel obliged to recognize a group with normally fatal incompatibilities just because of local issues of solidarity. Situations where A mutually recognizes B and B mutually recognizes C, but A and C do not recognize each other are common; even so, if Masons from both A and C are visiting B at the same time, the visitors could both find themselves in trouble when they go home. Despite this potential, Grand Lodges accept that other bodies sometimes have to come to expedient arrangements, and it isn't uncommon for D to refuse to recognize B because B accepts C.

Some Masonic researchers have tried to draw up a worldwide recognition map, but the scale of the job is so huge – and the exact details are forever changing, anyway – that it has not so far proven possible. Most Grand Lodges draw the line at maintaining a list of other Grand Lodges that they consider regular. Some go a little further and also note the main decisions made by those other regular Grand Lodges, but almost none wastes members' money on investigating what irregular (and, therefore, forbidden) institutions are up to.

The issue of visiting and regularity is what lies behind the common mistaken impression that Freemasonry is for men only. There are indeed male-only "jurisdictions" (the sphere of influence and power of a given Grand Lodge), but there are also female-only jurisdictions, and mixed-sex jurisdictions as well. Because granting recognition includes granting access to lodge meetings, it is not possible for the single-sex Grand Lodges to grant recognition to their opposing numbers, or to the mixed-sex groups. If they did so, they would be breaking the single-sex requirement – which was originally put in place, like the bar on religion and politics, to try to head off internal division. Freemasonry is no more sexist than the school education system, which also includes single-sex male, single-sex female and mixed-sex institutions.

The false impression that only men can be Freemasons is entirely the result of lazy (or malicious) media reports that have confused a particular Grand Lodge's policy with Freemasonry as a whole. This is roughly similar to mistaking the Arizona Cardinals for the entire sport of American Football. In fact, the United Grand Lodge of England – which, as the oldest surviving Grand Lodge, is given a certain amount of unofficial respect by most other Grand Lodges – has recently released a statement agreeing that a pair of female single-sex Grand Lodges are to be judged regular in every respect save for their female membership: as glowing an endorsement as its own charter permits it to give.

Two of the most common reasons for refusing to recognize an otherwise regular Grand Lodge are territory clashes and quirks or peculiarities regarding the formation process. While nowadays the great majority of new Grand Lodges follow the rules of establishment very carefully and precisely, historical situations have often meant that long-established Grand Lodges have questionable standing because specific details aren't quite right.

The same goes for territory – history is often complex. During the original expansion of Freemasonry, existing Grand Lodges founded new lodges well outside their traditional territorial sphere. This was usually to meet the demands of expatriates and military personnel while abroad. In some territories, several different National Grand Lodges established extensive lodge networks, all competing with local lodges. Almost all of these situations have now been resolved, but there is still a number of lodges reporting back to Grand Lodges on different continents, and some strange boundaries have arisen in places.

To add to the territorial confusion, not everyone always agreed on where boundaries could be drawn. Where there was territory disputed by neighbouring states, sometimes Grand Lodges on both sides claimed the area. If, later, neither backed down, the territorial disagreement could be enough to have many other groups regard one or both sides as irregular. A Grand Lodge without clearly sovereign territory is not properly constituted in many eyes.

Similar issues could arise with previously irregular Grand Lodges wanting to come in from the cold. If a Grand Lodge changes one of its key tenets, it is likely to render itself irregular in some eyes, and regular in others.

Women have a long history of Masonic activity, going back at least as far as the seventeenth century according to some historians. Shown here is an early nineteenth-century rendering of the Masonic initiation ceremony of a lady Freemason.

For example, if a mixed-sex Grand Lodge split into two single-sex organizations, other mixed-sex organizations would no longer class it as regular, while other single-sex groups may well find that their gender's half was, indeed, now regular. However, the chances are that the newcomer would already be impinging on some other Grand Lodge's territory. When that sort of clash arises, it may be seen as desirable by some Grand Lodges to recognize the newcomer as well, while others may be less convinced. This issue has been a particularly thorny one for the Prince Hall Freemasonry movement, which we'll talk about shortly.

Variations of Freemasonry

As might be expected from considering the international situation of Freemasonry, there is quite a number of variations to be found within it, at all levels. Some of these have come about because of historical miscommunications or schisms, while others were innovations or updates that found partial success – enough to establish a working foundation, but not enough to become unique. Still more alterations happened because of attempts to get back to older roots.

The greatest potential for variation lies in the actual minutiae of the Symbolic Lodge rituals. There is a wide range of workings. Most Grand Lodges have a list of which ones are permissible, and which are not. Very few permit all as a blanket definition, because some of the more obscure workings are a very long way from regular Freemasonry – such as the largely discredited Swedenborg Rite, which rather eccentrically attempts to blend Masonic styling with Emmanuel Swedenborg's philosophical teachings. Some of the more common variations include Emulation, Taylor's, York (not to be confused with the set of appendant bodies of the same name), Sussex, Logic, Universal, South London, Bristol, London West End, French, Modern, Scots, Scottish Rectified, Schroeder's and Logic. Others that are considered disreputable or are thought to have fallen by the wayside include the Memphis-Misraim Rites (with up to 95 different degrees), the Ancient and Accepted Rite (with 90 degrees), the Hermetic Rite, the Martinist Rite and the Swedenborg.

Differences in ritual aside, the variances between common workings are subtle enough that anyone familiar with one will be comfortable with all, although the occasional difference in wording or procedure will crop up. For most Masons, the issue of jurisdiction and regularity is far more important, and this is the area that can cause serious trouble for a member. There are a few broad "families" of jurisdiction – two of them significantly larger than the rest – within which most Grand Lodges recognize most of their fellows, and few others from outside.

Anglo and Continental Masonry

The most prevalent family of Masonic institutions is known informally worldwide as Anglo Masonry, because its rules and constitutions stem from the historic work and expansion of the Grand Lodge of England. The oldest of the Grand Lodges, the Grand Lodge of England was formed in 1717 (initially as the Grand Lodge of London), when four London lodges joined forces. Its regulatory focus started a few years later, and swiftly spread. In 1723, the first rule book was published. As the British Empire grew, it carried Masonry with it around the world. Over time, the various nations developed enough weight and history to stand on their own, and so formed their own sovereign Grand Lodges. After a period of schism in England, which saw two rival Grand Lodges active for just over a period of 60 years, the two combined into the current body, the United Grand Lodge of England, which is known worldwide by its initials, UGLE. Despite the assorted differences that creep in regionally, and natural national pride in the various sovereign bodies, UGLE retains a certain informal respect and status as the effective birthplace of modern Craft Masonry – in the Anglo branch, anyway.

The other large Masonic family of organizations is known as Continental Masonry, and traces its oldest jurisdiction back to the Grand Orient d'France, founded in 1733. Its relations with the rest of Masonry were perfectly regular up until 1868, when the Grand

Orient – which did not acknowledge the doctrine of sovereign territory that UGLE was so keen on – agreed to recognize a second Grand Lodge in Louisiana. The earlier Louisianan Grand Lodge complained extremely loudly and, by 1876, most of the English-speaking Grand Lodges had reclassified the Grand Orient as irregular. In 1877 the body further outraged English-speaking Masonry by removing the requirement for belief in a supreme being, making the presence of holy scripture optional in its lodges, and allowing women to visit lodge meetings. As you might expect, almost all the remaining English-language Grand Lodges severed ties immediately.

The Grand Orient wasn't without supporters, however, and continued to go about its business as it pleased. Many of the European Grand Lodges and Grand Orients followed its lead, which is why it is now known as Continental Masonry. It dominates Freemasonry in Europe and Latin America, while Anglo Masonry dominates in the English-speaking world. It is broadly true now, however, that most territories with an Anglo Grand Lodge also have an assigned Continental Grand Lodge or Orient – and vice versa.

The Prince Hall Movement

Aside from the big two, smaller jurisdictions have typically arisen where there were disagreements on the basics of admission policy. Prince Hall was a free-born African American who, along with 14 colleagues, was initiated into a Military Lodge under the jurisdiction of the Grand Lodge of Ireland in 1775. Military Lodges are mobile by nature, and when the lodge duly moved away, Hall and his fellows were given permission to continue meeting, but not to perform initiations.

In 1784, the group applied for a Warrant of Charter from the Grand Lodge of England, and formed African Lodge #459. In 1813, however, after the rectification of English Masonry, the newly formed UGLE moved address and withdrew a lot of its activities worldwide. African Lodge #459 was left with no means of contact with its former Grand Lodge, and was consequently removed from the UGLE rolls for non-payment of dues.

With nowhere else to turn, African Lodge restyled itself African Grand Lodge #1 (not to be confused with

Despite the differences in rite and ritual, Masonic lodge rooms tend to follow broadly the same pattern, as seen here.

African-American members of a US Grand Lodge assembled for a group photograph, just before the turn of the twentieth century.

any of the Grand Lodges in Africa, of course) and continued operating. The widespread racism at the time made it very difficult for African Americans to achieve membership in white-dominated lodges, and the movement – now known as Prince Hall Freemasonry – flourished. It remains very strong today. Although considered ritually regular, the Prince Hall Grand Lodges are only slowly being accepted as regular bodies.

There are two big stumbling blocks that the Prince Hall movement faces for recognition, and neither of them has anything to do with racism any more, save perhaps in a very few intransigent areas in the deep south of the USA. One is that the formation of African Grand Lodge #1 was undoubtedly irregular and, under Masonic canon, that means the other Grand Lodges it has created are also irregular; the other is that the Prince Hall Grand Lodges all impinge on the sovereign territory of older Grand Lodges. However, it is also

widely recognized that Prince Hall Masonry developed because there was nowhere else for its brothers to turn at the time. The Prince Hall Grand Lodges are slowly winning acceptance across Anglo Freemasonry, bit by bit – UGLE currently recognizes some, but not all – and it seems just a matter of time before they are entirely regularized.

Masonry for Women

When Freemasonry first developed – in the eighteenth century – there was a tacit assumption among its members that women just wouldn't be interested. There are a couple of early records of fully regular lodges with female members, and one of the earliest forms of the ritual workings includes the designation "He or She" in reference to the candidate, but, for the most part, the women of the time were too downtrodden to factor. The nineteenth century was the real flourishing of society-

Female Masons at Caxton Hall, London, in 1937: female jurisdictions are a full and vitally important part of Freemasonry worldwide.

wide sexism, though, and as that time approached the requirement that Freemasons be male was recognized as a formal Landmark.

When the Grand Orient d'France reorganized its charter in 1877, it indicated to all parties that it was all right to be separate from "regular" Masonry. Two international mixed-sex jurisdictions were formed fairly swiftly, called Le Droit Humain and the Order of International Co-Masonry. Both are still fully active worldwide. The Grand Orient and all affiliated Continental Grand Lodges swiftly granted them full recognition, along with any national female-only Grand Lodges that sprang up. A completely separate, but similarly aimed women's organization called the Order of Weavers developed and that, too, has spread.

Anglo Freemasonry still does not formally recognize female or mixed-sex Grand Lodges on the grounds that it would mean breaking charter; the resistance to such a

move is now concentrated in North America. However, UGLE openly accepts that female and mixed-sex jurisdictions are indeed a full part of Freemasonry, just not under the UGLE banner. Their announcement, in March 1999, plainly states "Freemasonry is not confined to men", with just the simple proviso that "this Grand Lodge does not itself admit women". Two female Grand Lodges based in England – the Honourable Fraternity of Ancient Freemasons (which is becoming international, with lodges in Spain and Gibraltar) and the Order of Women's Freemasons – and one mixed-sex Grand Lodge have been recognized by UGLE as fully regular, apart from the sex of their membership; a declaration that may well herald the approach of full recognition. Note also that the two female groups and the mixed-sex group do not formally recognize each other, for the same reasons of charter. All the groups are in regular informal contact on matters of mutual concern. There are Women's Grand

Lodges in many European countries. In North America, Women's Freemasonry is still meeting resistance. Rather than joining a female jurisdiction – the Women's Grand Lodge of Belgium has four lodges in the USA – it is more common for interested women to join a group called the Order of the Eastern Star, which is open to Masons and to women who are related to a male Mason.

There are scores of other tiny, self-styled Grand Lodges. Some of these appear to be protest movements against a specific policy of a mainstream Grand Lodge, and tend to be short-lived; others are active scams, degree mills designed to milk money out of prospective Masons. In general, if a supposedly Masonic body is not recognized by any Grand Lodge within Anglo, Continental, Prince Hall Freemasonry and Co-Masonry/Women's Freemasonry, it should be treated with extreme caution.

Symbolic Masonry

The great majority of all Masonic activity falls under the broad category of what is known as Symbolic Freemasonry, and in others as Blue Lodge or Craft Freemasonry. Symbolic Lodges are, simply, what most people think of when they think of a Masonic lodge – a locally organized group, presided over by the Worshipful Master and his officers, that initiates new members into Freemasonry and discusses local and internal matters. These are the lodges that make up most of Freemasonry and, for many members, represent the limit of their Masonic interests.

There are only three true ranks within Freemasonry – Entered Apprentice (first degree), Fellowcraft (second degree) and Master Mason (third degree). Although all sorts of other teaching degrees exist – more on that in a minute – they carry no authority or ranked weight. The

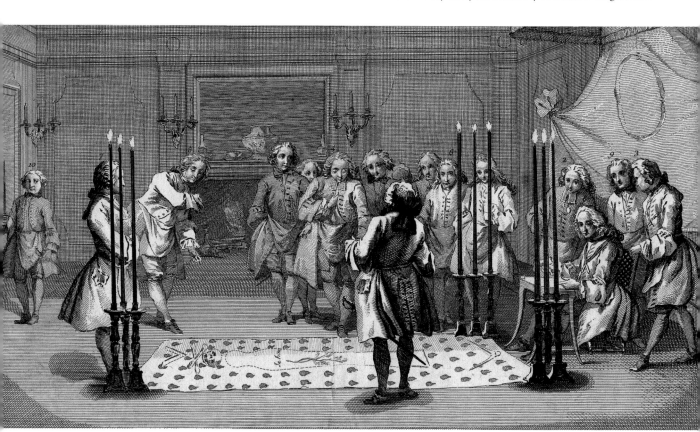

A group of Master Masons prepare their lodge room for the ceremony of raising a candidate to the third degree.

Worshipful Master of a lodge is, of course, the head of that lodge, and is due respect accordingly, but he is still a Master Mason, and any Master Mason may potentially reach that position. It is one of the Landmarks of Freemasonry that all Master Masons are equal, irrespective of any further teachings they may undergo.

A candidate starts Masonic life as a petitioner, outside the organization entirely. Everyone's first experience of Freemasonry is the ceremony in which they are initiated into the first degree, that of Entered Apprentice. This degree's ritual (and the one after it) draw on imagery of life as a worker helping to build King Solomon's temple. It teaches the new Freemason that it is important to labour on building the temple of his good character and to master his emotions in favour of his morality. Obedience to rules and regulations is stressed. After the ceremony has been completed, the new Entered Apprentice is allowed to take part in those parts of lodge meetings that are not restricted to higher ranks – specifically, second- and third-degree initiation ceremonies, and Master-only business. It varies, of course, but many lodges consider that Entered Apprentices are not yet proven enough to be entitled to vote in some or all lodge decisions. Additionally, in many lodges it is expected that the newest member of the lodge will selflessly volunteer to do any chores that the lodge requires.

When the lodge feels the member is ready and has proven genuinely interested and reliable, the second-degree initiation ceremony will take place. This raises the Apprentice to the rank of Fellowcraft. As a symbolic skilled workman, the Fellowcraft is introduced to the tools by which he can understand the world and his place within it – the five senses, the orders of architecture, the

A dramatic moment during the third-degree ceremony. After the ritual, the candidate will be a fully fledged Master Mason.

principles of geometry and the seven liberal arts and sciences. Again, the exact details vary from lodge to lodge, but generally a Fellowcraft will only have to leave the lodge room for third-degree initiation ceremonies, will be entitled to vote on all lodge matters and should be fairly safe from having to run any errands. After a further time, which depends entirely on the lodge's discretion, the Fellowcraft will be initiated into the third degree – becoming a Master Mason.

Once a member has attained the "supreme and exalted" rank of third-degree Master Mason, the highest rank attainable, the entire society is accessible. The degree draws on the legend of the murder of Solomon's chief architect in the construction of his temple in Jerusalem, and teaches the candidate that he must not cheat, defraud or wrong his fellows, and that he must render aid and assistance where required. The temple is incomplete, and its construction inside the self is the work of a lifetime. A Master Mason may serve as one of the lodge's officers; may visit any other (approved) lodge, subject to invitation; may take full part in Lodges of Research and Instruction; and may seek deeper learning

This highly allegorical and symbolic illustration is meant to depict the interior of the perfect lodge room, as constructed within the soul of each true Freemason.

and instruction by joining one or more of the appendant teaching bodies. None of these is actually required of any member, of course – although all are encouraged – and none carries any extra ranking. There are plenty of steps to take from that of Master Mason, down a fair number of different paths, but they are all sideways steps.

The Lodge Room
It is important to emphasize that a lodge is a gathering of Masons rather than the hall in which they have their meeting, which is specifically the lodge room. Lodge rooms come in all sorts of different styles – which should be no surprise by now – from the minimalist to the opulent. However, they do share certain features. All lodge rooms should be aligned east–west, with lockable doors at the west end, and a raised seat for the Master of the lodge at the east end. There should be seats or benches for the members along the north and south

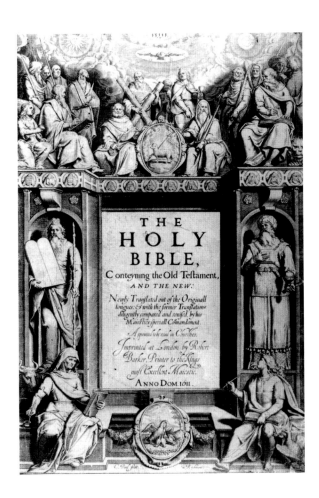

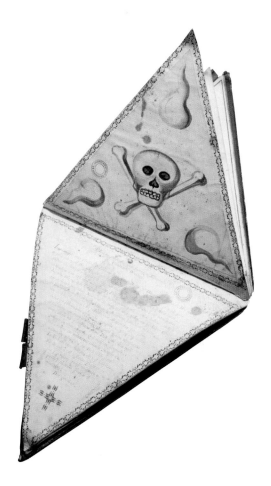

The King James Bible is the typical Christian masonic first choice to serve as the Volume of the Sacred Law.

This grade certificate from eighteenth-century France depicts a skull and crossbones, perhaps as a warning against thieves.

walls, separated into easterly and westerly groups. The Senior Warden and Junior Warden require seats and benches, to the south and the west, respectively.

The ceiling, which represents the heavens, may have some solar decoration or imagery on it; the floor, which represents earth, traditionally includes an area of black-and-white checkering or other mosaic. Somewhere on display there should be a design, known as a Tracing Board, which illustrates the principles of one of the three degrees – the appropriate board is presented depending on which degree of Mason the meeting is restricted to. Most lodge rooms will also have displayed (or carefully preserved close to hand) their certificate from Grand Lodge warranting their formation. This is a particular source of pride for older lodges.

Most importantly of all, though, the "furnishings" of the lodge have to be on display. Without them, there can be no lodge meeting. These vital items – the three Great Lights of Freemasonry – are the book of holy scripture

that the lodge chooses to recognize (known as the Volume of the Sacred Law), the square, and the compass. Their light is said to be embodied in the lodge's three senior officers, the Worshipful Master, the Senior Warden and the Junior Warden. In Christian countries, the Volume of the Sacred Law is usually the King James translation of the Bible; however, it can just as easily be the Torah, the Koran, the Vedas, the Zend-Avesta or any other holy scripture that reflects the religion of the members. There is also a great number of other symbolic and representational devices that are found at every well-established lodge. The precise details of the lodge room's symbolic contents and their meanings will be the subject of later sections.

Lodge Officers

A lodge may meet with a minimum of three members to discuss business, but rituals and initiations are all performed by seven of the lodge's officers (or their temporary stand-ins). In addition to these seven ritual posts, there are eight (or more) positions that do not typically take part in rituals. Any lodge with less than seven Master Masons in attendance is forbidden from performing initiations, and if all three of the senior officers are missing it cannot open at all. Each of the officers has a set of very precise duties and requirements, and it is fairly common for members interested in taking office to progress through the ritual offices in order, from Junior Steward all the way up to Worshipful Master.

The Tyler, or Outer Guard, is the external face of the lodge. This is the person who stands outside and guards the closed doors of the lodge room against eavesdroppers, intruders and, for symbolic reasons, lions and other wild beasts. The Tyler's symbol is a sword, and represents each Mason's vigilance against unworthy actions or thoughts. The Tyler's duties include maintaining and preparing lodge paraphernalia before meetings, helping the Senior Deacon to welcome visitors, ensuring that all attending Masons are properly attired, logging all entrants to the lodge room, standing outside on guard for the duration of the meeting, and finally tidying up and putting away the paraphernalia afterward. Because the Tyler never gets to take part in meetings, it is quite common for a lodge to appoint an experienced volunteer from a different lodge to this post.

The Inner Guard is the Tyler's counterpart inside the lodge room. When ritual calls for a check to ensure that the Tyler is vigilant and on guard outside, it is the Inner Guard's duty to communicate with the Tyler via a series of knocks. The Inner Guard collects candidates for initiation when they enter the lodge and delivers them to the Junior Deacon. Additionally, the Inner Guard is supposed to make significant progress learning the rituals of initiation, as preparation for further roles.

The Junior Deacon serves as the messenger of the Senior Warden. He also makes sure that nobody leaves or enters the lodge room without the permission of the Worshipful Master or Senior Warden once it is in session. Duties of the post include helping to prepare candidates going through an initiation, along with understudying the Senior Deacon's role in ceremonies so that he can fill in if necessary. The Junior Deacon is also expected to study the lodge's constitutions and by-laws at length.

The Senior Deacon is the messenger of the Worshipful Master. His role is to welcome visiting Masons and to introduce them to other lodge members, making sure the ice is well broken. He also prepares the ballot box when a vote requires it. The Senior Deacon has a fairly active role in initiations, including conducting candidates around the lodge during the ceremony, jogging the candidate's memory if appropriate, and delivering a particular lecture at the appropriate ritual point. It is expected that the Senior Deacon will make time to attend one or more "Lodges of Instruction" during his duty, and that he will also learn the Worshipful Master's part of the first-degree initiation ceremony.

The Junior Warden is tasked with coordinating lodge activities. As the third-in-command in the lodge hierarchy, he has more time available than the Senior Warden or the Worshipful Master, and so tends to be the one to whom members turn when they need help. His tasks include taking the role of Master if for some reason both the Worshipful Master and Senior Warden are away, and, by obvious extension, learning the ritual of lodge business. This includes opening and closing the lodge, conferring initiations and carrying out other regular business. He is also expected to help the Senior Warden with any special duties, and to help in other ways, such as supervising the lodge at its refreshment, and arranging the details of visits both to and from other lodges.

The Senior Warden is the Worshipful Master's primary assistant in the matter of governing the lodge. It is customary in many lodges for the officers to rotate upward on a yearly basis, so the Senior Warden has a year to learn all the things needed to prepare for his turn as Master. The Senior Warden is expected to be able to fill in for the Worshipful Master as necessary in any lodge business, from conferring degrees to closing the lodge. He is also supposed to be fully up to speed with the activities of the lodge committees (if any), how all the prospective membership and prospective officers stand, the lodge finances, and the full details of lodge procedure, jurisdiction and so on. It is a responsible position, and one that entails a lot of learning if the Senior Warden is going to be successful as Worshipful Master the following year.

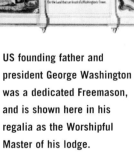

US founding father and president George Washington was a dedicated Freemason, and is shown here in his regalia as the Worshipful Master of his lodge.

The Worshipful Master of a Masonic lodge in continental India, complete with several badges and insignia of rank on his Masonic collar.

The **Worshipful Master** is the most senior of all the lodge's officials, and is devoted to maintaining the lodge in good order. In addition to having a large role in all initiation ceremonies – and having to memorize copious amounts of text for them – the Master also presides over the lodge, maintaining harmony, controlling discussion and opening and closing the lodge as appropriate. Other duties include selecting the lodge officers for the year (or running the vote for such positions as are decided by the lodge), approving the lodge's financial activities, liaising with Grand Lodge on behalf of the lodge, keeping in touch with all members and so on.

The **Junior Steward** is the most junior of the non-ceremonial officers, and the position that carries least responsibility in the lodge. As the designation "non-ceremonial" suggests, neither Steward takes part in any aspect of lodge ritual; rather, their efforts are focused on helping out before and after meetings. The Junior Steward's specific job is to assist the Senior Steward, although it is expected that he will provide assistance to the Junior Warden when the lodge is taking refreshment, help any visiting Masons to take care of any reasonable needs that they might have, and to help the Tyler prepare new candidates. Most of all, though, the Junior Steward should be trying to prove fitness for higher office through cheerful assistance, regular and punctual attendance, general enthusiasm and willingness to learn, and beginning efforts to start learning the rituals of the three degrees. In large lodges, the Junior Steward may be assigned a Junior Junior Steward as an assistant.

The **Senior Steward** endeavours to provide general assistance to the other officers of the lodge in the discharge of their duties – between meetings as well as during lodge sessions. As such, an active lodge can keep the Senior Steward quite busy over the course of his time. During lodge meetings, as well as helping to ensure that everything runs smoothly and all visitors are comfortably seated, the Senior Steward ensures that the dining tables are properly arranged and furnished at refreshment, and that every member has everything that he needs.

The **Chaplain** is entrusted with the care of the Volume of the Sacred Law. As well as ensuring the wellbeing of the book, his main duty lies in opening and closing all meetings with a religiously universal prayer, in keeping

This emblem – referred to as a jewel – would have been worn by a Mason attending a Stewards' Grand Lodge meeting.

with regular Masonic practice. He is also required to learn the scriptural lessons associated with each degree, so that he is able to recite them when necessary. Finally, he must attend all Masonic funeral services and offer the prayers at that service.

The **Almoner** ensures the lodge maintains contacts with all its members. The officer in charge of providing a link between the active members and Masons who – because of illness, bad fortunes or other adverse circumstances – are unable to attend meetings, he also provides a point of first contact for any member in genuine distress who needs some guidance, moral support, or material help, and keeps in touch with former members' widows. It is the Almoner's duty to bring the lodge's attention to sick or needy members, and to make whatever arrangements are deemed suitable. If charitable assistance is appropriate, the Almoner will deal with the correct charities.

The **Charity Steward**, by comparison, is responsible for overseeing the lodge's charitable activities. In addition to regular collections made during lodge meetings, it is usual for the Charity Steward to organize other programmes and drives, bring appropriate events to members' attentions and even, if time permits and the lodge agrees, to organize external events. He also deals with the various charities to which the lodge contributes directly, and although all funds will go through the Secretary and Treasurer as usual, the Charity Steward directs the disbursement of monies to the various causes.

The **Treasurer** serves specifically as the lodge's banker. For this reason, a working knowledge of good business practices is important for the office, and a little accounting experience can be very advantageous. The Treasurer's duties include collecting money from the Secretary and investing it properly as per the lodge's will, paying out funds when ordered by the Worshipful Master with the consent of the lodge, preparing regular statements of account and maintaining scrupulous and exact documentation of all finances and transactions.

The **Immediate Past Master**, as the name suggests, is the person who served as Worshipful Master immediately before the current office-holder. His duty is simply to advise the Worshipful Master if and when requested, and to provide him with other guidance or assistance that he might ask for. The IPM, as he is generally known, is not allowed to take the Worshipful Master's place in case of the Master's absence – only the Senior and Junior Wardens are so entitled. If all three officers are missing, the lodge cannot meet.

The **office of Secretary** carries a number of very important administrative duties, and the post requires a high degree of trust and responsibility. As the administrator of the lodge's affairs, the Secretary has to record minutes of all lodge proceedings, maintain the register of members, prepare regular reports for the lodge and for Grand Lodge, disseminate information as required and so on. Typically, the Secretary should attempt to be early for meetings so that there is time to prepare everything. The Secretary is the first point of

contact for communications into and out of the lodge, so has to be able to act as the lodge's ambassador, with all that entails. Along with maintaining full and orderly files of all lodge papers, records, vouchers, receipts and other documents, the Secretary is also responsible for collecting dues and other monies paid to the lodge, passing them to the Treasurer, and issuing all appropriate receipts. The post involves a lot of work, and large lodges may appoint an Assistant Secretary. Alternatively, the Secretary may call on the Stewards for help when appropriate.

As acting adjutant to the Worshipful Master, the **Director of Ceremonies** is exempt from certain lodge protocol, even during rituals. His duty is to make sure that all lodge activity is carried out with due propriety and that rituals run smoothly. This is an extremely exacting role, and the Director of Ceremonies needs to have memorized flawlessly not only every aspect – physical as well as verbal – of each ritual, initiation and lesson, but also to be expert in the relative respects and honours accorded to members and visitors according to their experience and the roles they may have within Grand Lodge. It is common for each lodge to be regularly visited by various duly-appointed officers of the Grand Lodge, all of whom are due considerable respect. Things can rapidly become complicated, and the Director of Ceremonies needs to be entirely fluent in the etiquette and jurisprudence of the Grand Lodge. The Director of Ceremonies has the ultimate responsibility for the readiness of the lodge before the meeting begins, for correctly seating visitors according to their status, for ensuring that the lodge's ceremonial officers are in the right place at the right points and for making sure that rituals go smoothly. Should he notice an error or omission – or a member having trouble with lines – he has to step in discreetly and diplomatically, and put matters to right. The Director of Ceremonies is assumed at all times to be acting as the Worshipful Master's voice, and is immediately obeyed, but the role requires quiet dignity rather than arrogance – it is disastrous for a Director of Ceremonies to try to rule the lodge. This is one of the most demanding of all positions in the lodge, and usually falls to a highly experienced Past Master (a former Worshipful Master), or to a member with eidetic memory, if such is available.

Further Developments

In addition to progressing through the ranks of the lodge's officers, a Master Mason is also free to join an appendant body or other related group. These are designed to allow the Master Mason to continue moral development and progression without in any way replacing the core lodge work. There are several different options available – depending, of course, on the territory the Mason is active in. By far and away the most important of these appendant bodies are the Scottish Rite and the York Rite, roughly parallel systems that provide further scope for learning and development. Although both the York and Scottish Rites award further degrees (with increasing numeric value), they both place great emphasis on the sideways nature of their work, agreeing absolutely that the third is the highest-ranking degree any Mason can attain.

The York Rite

Providing a framework for Master Masons to continue their moral and spiritual development after they have attained the third degree in Blue Lodge Masonry, the York Rite expands the historical and mythic background

Templer.

of Freemasonry, and attempts to give greater meaning to the Craft. While it is still not a religion, it does develop themes based on the medieval crusades, and part of its workings are specifically Christian in tone.

There are generally held to be four separate bodies within the York Rite, which, between them, can confer a further ten additional degrees after that of Master Mason. These are the familiar first three degrees of the Symbolic (also Craft or Blue) Lodge, the Holy Royal Arch (also known as the Chapter, the name given to a gathering of Royal Arch Masons, or Companions), the Council of Royal and Select Masters (also known as Cryptic Masonry) and the Commandery of Knights Templar. Advancing in degree in each requires no memorization, but each body offers plenty of opportunities to learn ritual workings as an officer, helping to convey the various degrees. Most of the ritual work of the York Rite is conveyed by officers playing a range of characters, robed and made up in order to add to the overall impact of the lessons they contain.

There is strong evidence to suggest that at one time the degree of Royal Arch Mason, the last of the Chapter's degrees, was actually part of the third degree. Certainly, the story presented by the first three degrees as it stands is incomplete, and the degrees of the Chapter, particularly the final one, go a long way toward bringing the tale to completion.

The oldest reference to Freemasonry in recorded text is to be found in the so-called Regius Poem, written in around AD 1390. It is almost 800 lines long and deals with a number of Masonic matters, referring to the late tenth century. Among the regulations and ethical proscriptions, it also recounts the legend of the city of York, from which the Rite gets its name. It is known that a man named Athelstan was King of England from AD 924–40. The grandson of Alfred the Great (who, incidentally, did not truly burn any cakes), he was the first king truly to govern all of England.

According to the Regius legend, Athelstan was an enthusiastic patron of Masonry and ordered the construction of many castles, forts and monasteries.

The tales and legends of the noble Knights Templar provided considerable inspiration for the founders of modern Freemasonry.

King Athelstan presents his charter to the very first Grand Lodge of Masons in AD 926.

He studied geometry and the liberal arts and, to preserve order, issued a "Charter of the Masons", by which they could hold a yearly meeting, in York. He apparently appointed his brother, Edwin, as the Grand Master, and the first Grand Lodge of Masons was supposedly held in 926. At that meeting, constitutions were established from documents written in many ancient languages, Greek, Latin and Hebrew included. Whether there is any truth to the poem or not is a moot point: it is interesting that such concepts can be dated back to 1390, let alone earlier.

The orders and degrees of the York Rite are undoubtedly much later developments than the Regius Poem, and there's little doubt that they accreted over time in different territories. The Chapter degree of Mark Master Mason was inspired by the practices of operative Freemasons in Germany in requiring each Mason to register an identifying mark, and it appears to have been invented in Scotland as early as 1676; meanwhile, the Chapter degree of Most Excellent Master seems to have

been an American innovation created more than a century later. However, by the time of the reformation of English Freemasonry in 1813, the York Rite was complete, and the Royal Arch, while recognized as part of the three degrees, was kept separate:

> *Pure Ancient Masonry is to consist of three degrees, and no more: viz., those of the Entered Apprentice, the Fellowcraft, and the Master Mason including the Supreme Order of the Holy Royal Arch.*
> United Grand Lodge of England, 1813

The second body in the York Rite, after the Symbolic Lodges, Royal Arch Masonry is governed by Supreme Grand Chapters, territorially equivalent to the Grand Lodges they are linked with. Meetings are held in local Chapters, each one traditionally associated with a specific Craft lodge that it originally came from. Its degrees invite

the candidate to consider his relationship with the divine, and are counted among the most impressive and profound ceremonies within the whole of Freemasonry. As with most Scottish Rite territories, the first degree awarded by the Royal Arch is numbered as fourth, although again none of the York Rite is seen as superior to the third degree of Craft Masonry.

The first of the Chapter degrees is the fourth degree of Mark Master Mason. Dating back as far as the tenth century, operative – in other words, professional – Masons have carved unique (later, in the fifteenth century, becoming registered) symbols into their work so that their buildings could be identified by their fellows, it is one of the degrees in Freemasonry with the greatest pedigree. Following on from the Fellowcraft degree, it teaches that although we may be misunderstood and underrated, we should be true to ourselves, stick to our duties and have the courage to defend that which we know is right. The truth will come to light if we keep faith in the supreme being. The degree uses the ritual setting of a simple labourer working in the temple quarries.

Every inch of this Scottish Rite Masonic Apron is covered in highly symbolic imagery. The pillars, for instance, represent the columns outside King Solomon's temple.

As an aside, it is important to note that some jurisdictions do not award a Mark Master Mason degree. Typically, these areas – the tradition is concentrated in the British Isles and, for historical reasons, in Ghana – require that a prospective member of the Chapter already be a Mark Master Mason. In order to fulfil this requirement, there is a separate York Rite body, called the Mark Master Masons, administered internationally by the Grand Lodge of Mark Master Masons of England and Wales and its Districts and Lodges Overseas. The organization meets in lodges and acts as the bridge between Symbolic and Chapter Masonry. To muddy the waters further, some lodges under the jurisdiction of the United Grand Lodge of England have special dispensation to award the degree of Mark Master Mason as the third degree of Symbolic Masonry, bypassing the requirement for its members to take the separate degree.

Solomon built the House of the Lord on the Mount where the Lord appeared to David his Father. II Chron. Ch. III. Ver. 1.

The Temple of Solomon.

The fifth degree is that of Virtual Past Master. This came about as something of a workaround to the initial requirement that only a Master Mason who had already been the Worshipful Master of his lodge was eligible to ascend to the Holy Royal Arch. The addition of this degree allowed all Master Masons to participate in the Chapter by teaching the pertinent lessons – namely, that you have to know how to obey before you can order, and to be able to rule yourself before you can expect to rule others. This degree does not carry the same status as being an actual Past Master, of course; it merely prepares the Mason for the Royal Arch. Its teachings also reinforce that Chapter-members (known as Companions) are obliged to bring knowledge and enlightenment to their less-informed fellows.

Most Excellent Master, the sixth degree, is an American innovation from late in the eighteenth century. Widely acknowledged as the most colourful and spectacular ceremony in Freemasonry, it is the only degree to draw on the imagery of the completion of Solomon's temple. Where, in all other degrees, the emphasis is on the

People have been speculating about the crypts beneath King Solomon's temple – and the wonders they may have held – for centuries.

necessity of striving to complete the work of building the temple – or seeking personal perfection – within the self, this degree is a foreshadowing of that potential.

The last of the Chapter degrees, the seventh, Royal Arch, is generally considered the culmination of the Symbolic degrees – the so-called "Root and Marrow" of Masonry. It draws on the imagery of the discovery of a crypt beneath the ruins of the temple, and the rediscovery of its greatest secrets. It is universally recognized as the most elegant and beautiful of all Masonic rituals, and tells the story of some of the darkest times in Jewish history – the enslavement of the Jewish people in Babylon after the destruction of Jerusalem and the temple. It culminates in the rediscovery of the Mason's Word. The degree teaches that there is light even in the greatest darkness, that the triumph of evil is temporary, and that those in faith are never truly alone.

The third body in the York Rite is the Council of Royal and Select Masters. It is also known as Cryptic Masonry – from its ritual emphasis on the contents of the mythic crypt beneath the temple ruins, rather than from any puzzling or hidden aspects of the Council. The Council degrees are known sometimes as the Degrees of Preservation or, affectionately, as the Three Little Jewels. The history of the Council degrees is complex and obscure, and the subject of much debate, but it is thought that they may have originated in France, with the Jacobite Scots exiles. They may have originally been part of the material that became the Scottish Rite, but if so were dropped along the way somewhere before becoming an independent body under the collective banner of the York Rite. If the Symbolic degrees represent the search for the Word, and the Chapter degrees represent its discovery, then the Council degrees could be said to represent its significance. Royal Arch Masons are entitled to progress to the Council.

The first of the Council degrees is that of Royal Master. Its symbolic imagery is that of a Fellowcraft who is seeking greater illumination. For his trials, he is eventually rewarded with secrets unknown to most of his fellows, symbolizing the core lesson that no matter what life throws at us, the faithful will earn eventual reward. However, once one's feet are on the path, it is not possible to turn aside. The greatest divine truths require a highly advanced personal spirituality genuinely to understand and perceive. By earning the prize that he has sought, the candidate is required to continue onward until perfection is attained, and he can truly own that which he has been given.

The next degree is the Select Master. Its rituals explain how the secrets found in the Royal Arch degree were preserved, and the candidate is given further teaching in the necessity for constant vigilance when dealing with life and the world, in order to avoid falling into unrighteousness. Only those who remain on guard have any hope of success. The key of the degree, however, is the emphasis of the point that all Masonic work is an allegory for the soul's search for truth. Dedication to this search is the Masonic work, and the work's completion is its reward. The First Temple, doomed to destruction, represents our earthly existence; the Second Temple, built on its foundations, will be our existence afterward. Only by striving to perfect our internal temple before its inevitable destruction can we hope to see our own Second Temple perfected.

The final degree of the Council is that of Super Excellent Master. Unlike its two fellows, it does not draw on the mythic imagery of the crypt, but instead looks at the errors and weaknesses that brought Solomon's successor to ruin and led to the destruction of Jerusalem. It teaches specifically that the unfaithful will be swallowed by catastrophe, no matter what their station – success is impossible without fidelity. As such, its candidates are exhorted always to walk in faith, remain true, and foster friendship.

The last section of the York Rite is the Commandery of Knights Templar. Uniquely among the recognized Masonic bodies, this body's rituals do have a specific religious connotation. Consequently, it is open only to Freemasons who believe in the Christian doctrine of the Trinity: the unity of Father, Son and Holy Ghost. The Commandery consists of three orders, named for the historical Knightly orders active in the Holy Land. Because of this, the Commandery is sometimes known as Chivalric Masonry. Commanderies are governed by an Eminent Commander, and overseen at a national level by their sovereign controlling body, the Grand Encampment of Knights Templar. The Commandery is not the same organization as the historical Templar order. This latter organization still exists, claiming an unbroken period of transmission continued in Scotland from the French suppression of 1312 onward. The order is still active today, expanding worldwide. If there are any Templar secrets to be had, they remain with the original Templars rather than with the Commandery.

The first order within the Commandery is the Illustrious Order of the Red Cross. This ceremony emphasizes the importance of truth, honesty and always keeping your promises. The ritual is split into two sections. The first is focused around Prince Zerubbabel's entry to the Jewish Council at Jerusalem. He wishes to borrow their authority so that he can visit Babylon to try to obtain permission from King Darius to use defensive force while rebuilding the ruined

Prince Zerubbabel, here
depicted in the red robe, was
largely responsible for the
historical efforts to reconstruct
King Solomon's temple.

Temple of Solomon. In the second section, Zerubbabel overcomes initial imprisonment to become friendly with the court of Darius, and takes part in a friendly contest, which he wins.

The second Commandery order is actually a combination of two – the Mediterranean Pass (or Order of St Paul) and the Order of Malta. The lessons in this order concentrate around the eight Beatitudes, symbolizing the eight-fold geometry of the Maltese Cross and the eight different languages once spoken by the historic membership of the Knights of Malta. The imagery of the ceremony is based around a knight who is about to set off to crusade. He is succoured on the island of Malta, receiving both food and spiritual enrichment to prepare him for the trials of his journey.

The Valiant and Magnanimous Order of the Temple completes the Commandery and the official York Rite. It tests and teaches faith, obligation, enthusiasm and humility, and reminds the candidate of his unstinting duty to help his fellows. The ceremony attempts to re-create a young knight's search for admission into

Gregorio Caraffa, an Italian, was Grand Master of the Knights of the Military Order of St John in Malta between 1680 and 1690.

the Templar order, along with the years of pilgrimage, penance and knightly service he is required to render. The lessons include dramatic and beautiful reminders of the death and ascension of Christ. Although the Commandery is the limit of York Rite Masonry, there is also a number of other appendant bodies, whose membership is drawn from members of the York Rite, and although there isn't space to go into the detail that they deserve, it is important at least to mention them.

The Masonic and Military Order of the Red Cross of Constantine, which meets in Conclaves and is governed by national United Grand Imperial Councils, is an invitation-only body with strictly limited membership, known as "Knights". Seen as the greatest honour available within the York Rite, its members are required to have demonstrated a very high level of dedication and performance in their Masonic activities. Prospective members, who must be Knights Templar in good standing, have to be nominated by a current member, and have to pass unanimous ballot. As such, this body is probably the closest equivalent that the York Rite has to the Scottish Rite's thirty-third degree. The order has three degrees, that of Knight, Priest-Mason and Prince-Mason. The historical order was founded by Constantine the Great in AD 312. No direct link is asserted to the traditional group, but the Red Cross of Constantine draws on the historic order's principles for its imagery.

Serving a slightly different purpose to the Red Cross of Constantine, the Knights of the York Cross of Honour are governed by a single body – the Convent General of the Knights of the York Cross of Honour. Membership is restricted to those dedicated individuals who have completed service as Worshipful Master of a Symbolic Lodge, High Priest of a Holy Royal Arch Chapter, Illustrious Master of a Cryptic Council of Royal and Select Masters, and Eminent Commander of a Commandery of Knights Templar. Candidates who meet this requirement then have to be sponsored by a current member and unanimously voted on. The further honour of Grand Cross of the Knights of the York Cross of Honour can be attained only by becoming the supreme presiding officer of one of the York Rite's four Grand bodies in that territory. The Knights of the York Cross of Honour specifically support leukaemia research.

St Helen, mother of Constantine, carrying the red cross that would become known by her son's name.

Noah and his family are
seen here hard at work on
the Ark. The Ark Mariners
celebrate their vision, piety
and prudence.

The organization of the Holy Royal Arch Knight Templar Priests is another invitational group. Past Masters of a Blue Lodge who also subscribe to a Royal Arch Chapter and a Templar Commandery are eligible for invitation to join a Tabernacle. Generally, sterling performance as the principal of a lodge or equivalent is considered good grounds for an invitation to be extended. The group is governed internationally by two sovereign Grand Colleges – the original in York, England, and a younger one in the USA dating from 1931.

The Holy Order of the Grand High Priest meets as a Tabernacle and is governed by Grand Councils. Candidates for membership as Excellent Companions have to be active High Priests of a Royal Arch Chapter. The Order's ceremony takes in the period from Melchizedek's blessing of Abram through to the consecration of Aaron the Levite as first Jewish High Priest. The initiates of the Holy Order are taught that they carry heavy responsibilities and duties, both as a Freemason and as a person, and that dedicated service to the supreme being and to society is the only way to discharge those responsibilities and duties.

The Order of the Allied Masonic Degrees dates to 1880. Its original Grand Council is headquartered at Mark Masons' Hall, the same building that houses the Grand Lodge of Mark Master Masons, mentioned earlier. There is also a sovereign Grand Council in the USA. Members of the Order have to be Mark Master Masons and Companions of the Royal Arch. Since 1931, when the degrees it controls were stabilized, the Order has conferred five Masonic Degrees. The first of these is St Lawrence the Martyr, which teaches fortitude. After that degree, members are free to take the remaining four degrees in any order they see fit, those being the Knights of Constantinople (which teaches humility), the Red Cross of Babylon (which explores Zerubbabel's life), the Grand Tylers of Solomon (which warns against carelessness and snap judgements), and the Grand High Priest (which looks at the consecration of Aaron). With an amazing 60 per cent increase in the number of Councils worldwide in the last 20 years, the Order is probably the fastest-growing body in Freemasonry today.

Last, but not least, as one of the more tenuously linked side degrees of the York Rite, the Ancient and

Scottish Rite aprons differ significantly from the less decorated, square aprons of the York Rite.

Honourable Fraternity of Royal Ark Mariners is open only to Mark Master Masons. With no direct correspondence to any of the other imagery employed within Freemasonry, the body is somewhat unique in the Masonic world. As the name suggests, its imagery is drawn from Noah's construction of the Ark and the lead-up to the great flood. Its ceremony draws analogies between the flood and real life to warn the Mark Master Mason of the dangers waiting in the world, and how we should strive to find our place of safety and rest. For historical reasons, the Royal Ark Mariners are administered internationally by the Grand Masters Royal Ark Council, under the jurisdiction of the Grand Lodge of Mark Master Masons.

The Scottish Rite

Clearly designed to extend the teachings of Craft Freemasonry (which it refers to as Symbolic), the Scottish Rite teaches a series of moral and spiritual degrees numbered from fourth up to the thirty-second. There is one further degree within the Scottish Rite, the famous thirty-third degree, which is awarded solely to selected thirty-second degree Masons who have rendered some special outstanding service to Freemasonry or the Scottish Rite body in particular, or who are judged to have lived lives that truly aspire to the best of the fellowship of mankind under the guidance of the divine. It is not possible to apply for the thirty-third degree, and recipients have to be 33 years old at the very least.

The Scottish Rite is governed by Supreme Councils. These operate in much the same way as Grand Lodges, except that they clearly recognize that any given Grand Lodge is the sole authority over Freemasonry in the lodges it controls. The Supreme Councils claim jurisdiction only over the working of the Scottish Rite and its meeting groups, known as "Valleys". A new Scottish Rite Mason joins a Valley, and there learns the lessons and degrees of the Rite, up to the thirty-second degree, in a manner parallel to Blue Lodge Masonry.

The Supreme Council is governed by a group known as the Active Members. Each separate district within the Supreme Council is overseen by a Deputy, who is the Rite's senior officer for that territory. The Deputy is assisted by the other Active Members from his territory. The number varies, but is always at least one. The Supreme Council meets once a year, to oversee the strategy and business of the Rite, and to hold the thirty-third degree ceremony for those chosen to receive the honour.

Despite being known as the Scottish Rite, the earliest references to the system appear in French records. It is referred to in these documents as "Rite Ecossais", which is where it takes its name – *Ecosse* is the French word for Scotland. France was host to a great many refugee Scots during the late seventeenth century, fleeing English oppression. Undoubtedly, there would have been a number of Masons among them, and it is possible that these refugee Masons were responsible for (or at least involved in) the creation of the Scottish Rite system.

The first Scottish Rite lodge can be traced back to the French city of Bordeaux in 1732. Over the next few years, the advanced degrees of the Rite were developed. By the time the Rite spread out of the country to the French territories in the West Indies, in 1763, they consisted of a system of 25 degrees known as the Rite of Perfection. Extra degrees were added until the modern structure of 33 degrees was complete, with the first three degrees being considered parallel and equivalent to the three degrees of the regular Craft. There are still a few Scottish Rite bodies that teach their own versions of the first three degrees, which are considered an acceptable regular variant by most Craft (Symbolic) Grand Lodges, but in most territories now the Blue Lodges are left to deal with the symbolic degrees.

The Scottish Rite particularly flourished in the USA. In 1801, the world's first Supreme Council of the Ancient and Accepted Scottish Rite was founded in South Carolina. Its goal was to gather the assorted Scottish Rite bodies in the USA together and to bring some sort of

order to the system, which at that time was chaotic. Of the 11 initial members of the Supreme Council – all holders of the thirty-third degree – just two were born in the USA, and their religious affiliations were similarly diverse; two were Roman Catholic, four Jewish and five Protestant. A similar body was formed in New York in 1813 with similar aims for the Northern section of the United States. Progress was slow in both halves of the country, thanks to a number of confounding factors, but eventually the two Supreme Councils brought the rest of the country into the fold.

As a result of these efforts, the Scottish Rite is now officially agreed as having been founded with the South Carolina Supreme Council in 1801. There are Supreme Councils worldwide, most of which have friendly relations with each other. Over one million Masons in the USA alone are affiliated with the Scottish Rite, and approximately 10,000 of them have reached the rank of thirty-third degree. As mentioned before, the Supreme Council and its subordinate bodies do not claim any status higher than that of any other Master Mason, and fully acknowledge the Craft Grand Lodges as superior. The Grand Master of Masons – the title given to the head of Grand Lodge – is unquestioningly recognized as the highest-ranking officer present should he attend any Scottish Rite meeting.

The ranks of the Scottish Rite are broken into four divisions. While there is some variance in specific detail, depending on where in the world you are – as there is with most of Freemasonry – the lessons of each degree remain strikingly consistent. The four divisions are commonly referred to as the Lodge of Perfection, which refers to the degrees from the fourth to the fourteenth. The first ten of these are referred to as the Ineffable Degrees, leading up to the Degree of Perfection. The Chapter of Rose Croix then takes the candidate from the fifteenth to the eighteenth degree, the Council of Kadosh from nineteenth to the thirtieth, and the Consistory administers the last two degrees, the thirty-first and the thirty-second. To give some idea of the potential variance, though, the northern USA and Canada follows the Lodge of Perfection with the Council of Princes of Jerusalem for the fifteenth and sixteenth degrees, then the Chapter of Rose Croix for seventeenth and eighteenth degrees, while classifying everything from

PRAECEPIT REX SALOMON VT TOLLERENT LAPIDES GRANDES LAPIDES PRECIOSOS
IN FVNDAMENTVM TEMPLI ET QVADRARENT EOS Reg.III.C.
Raph. Sanct. pin:
N.˚ XLVIII

This painting shows
stonemasons of all grades
hard at work building King
Solomon's temple, while
Solomon himself consults
with Hiram Abiff.

The beauty of Solomon's temple was so great that even the angels were transfixed by its splendour and lavish wonder.

the nineteenth degree up as the Consistory. In addition, several of the individual degree titles differ by territory.

The first of the Ineffable Degrees, the fourth, confers the title of Secret Master, and it teaches the importance of duty and fidelity, the necessity for secrecy in confidential matters, personal integrity and due silence when appropriate. Its rituals relate to the story of King Solomon's temple, and particularly to his appointment of seven expert Masons to guard the holy of holies and its sacred furniture.

The fifth degree is that of the Perfect Master. Its lesson is that we are all mortal and must pay respect to those who have passed before. It also re-emphasizes that honesty and trustworthiness are at the base of all Masonic honour, and therefore should be a primary concern in anything a Mason does. Impure thoughts and unworthy ambitions are corrupting and lead to moral and spiritual destruction. Its ritual setting relates to the murder of Hiram Abiff, the legendary architect of Solomon's temple, who plays a central role in the mythology of Freemasonry.

The sixth degree carries the title of Intimate Secretary. It draws on a tale of King Solomon saving the life of a Mason mistaken for a spy and eavesdropper to teach a lesson about faithfulness, devotion and zeal – particularly that Masons should take great care to avoid prying into the personal business of their fellows, in order to avoid situations that may cause offence.

Justice and impartiality are the main themes of the seventh degree, called Provost and Judge. It affirms that just one law must apply to all people equally and without favour – but tempered with warranted mercy. Its ritual tells of King Solomon appointing several different judges to hear the case against Hiram Abiff's presumed murderers.

Intendant of the Building is the title given to the eighth degree. The word "intendant" indicates a less-responsible position than that of Superintendent. This degree teaches the importance of charity and benevolence and stresses that all Masons should take it upon themselves to educate the orphaned, support the distressed, succour the ill and comfort the aged. Honours are a step toward perfection. The ritual of this degree is about how Solomon got work restarted on the temple after the death of his architect.

The ninth degree, Elect of the Nine, is cautionary. The title refers to Solomon's selection of nine Masons to investigate the earlier murder. The message of this is that we all need to remain cautious at all times to make sure that we do not get so carried away by a cause we feel strongly about that our actions start to become unrighteous. If you look for common ground between religions, you find it in the universal teachings of providing loving service to the community and people around you. That should be your guide.

Following on directly from the previous degree, the tenth degree teaches that fanatical behaviour and belief will never defeat equal justice and universal freedom. Justice will always wait to punish transgressors against society and its members, no matter how strongly they believe they were "just doing the right thing". Its title, Elect of the Fifteen, reflects its continuance of the previous lesson with reference to the fifteen Masons who sought the prosecution of the architect's murderers.

The two previous degrees are brought to completion with the eleventh degree, Elect of the Twelve, which reminds us that virtuous behaviour is rewarded just as much as evil is punished. It shows that the true and faithful will gain rich rewards for their goodness sooner or later, and exhorts all Masons to be honest, sincere and earnest in their dealings. Its ritual reinforces this message, describing the rewards given to twelve of the fifteen prosecuting Masons.

The twelfth degree is that of the Grand Master Architect. It teaches the Mason to contemplate the world and his place within it, and to treat it as a child of the divine. This is accomplished through reference to the lessons of a training school established for the builders involved in the construction of the temple, and to the specific instruments and tools involved in the trade.

As the penultimate degree within the Lodge of Perfection and the last Ineffable Degree, the thirteenth degree, the Royal Arch of Solomon, is a preparation for the final culminating "degree of perfection". Its lessons are that a true and faithful person will not be deterred from the road to perfection by danger or difficulty. The very finest of life's experiences are to be attained only through hard, dedicated and frequently painful work.

The Lodge of Perfection culminates with the fourteenth degree of Grand Elect Perfect and Sublime Mason. This title represents the belief that the Mason now has all the tools required to prepare a spiritual Lodge of Perfection within himself. This room represents the secret vault under the holy of holies in Solomon's temple, which contained the so-named pillar of beauty. This pillar was said to bear the Tetragrammaton, the true four-letter name of God, which is revealed and explained during the degree ritual.

The series of degrees from the fifteenth to the eighteenth is known as the Chapter of Rose Croix. Its first lesson is that it is vital to be true to your own personal convictions, and to strive to do right. Over the course of the fifteen degrees, Knight of the East or Sword, the Biblical tale of the Babylonian captivity is told. Under the direction of King Cyrus, the Jewish captives in Babylon were taken back to Jerusalem, where they helped to build the Second Temple.

The sixteenth degree follows on directly from the previous one, continuing the story of the trials involved in the Second Temple's construction. The difficulties were such that Prince Zerubbabel of Jerusalem had to order the builders to work with their trowels in one hand and a sword in the other. The lesson of this degree, called Prince of Jerusalem, is that one has to remain loyal to the truth and to discharge one's duty with all due fidelity.

Knight of the East and West, the seventeenth degree, teaches that every person's primary allegiance should be to the divine, because the works of mankind are flawed, and will not last. Indeed, "temporal" and "temporary" come from the same root. The lesson to be drawn is that the only lasting place to build the Third Temple is within the hearts of humanity and that it should be constructed and dedicated to the divine.

The last degree within the Chapter of Rose Croix is that of Knight Rose Croix, the eighteenth degree. For the Mason in search of ultimate truth, the principles of faith, hope and charity are the guiding principles that will carry him forward on the journey. By carrying a temple for the divine within his heart, he will reaffirm the ideals of love, tolerance and universality by which the world could be transformed.

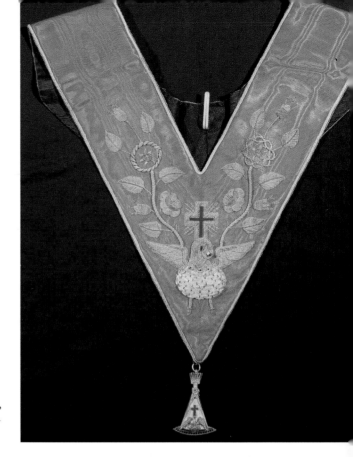

This ceremonial collar is worn by Scottish Rite Masons who have attained the level of eighteenth degree, Knight Rose Croix.

The degrees from the nineteenth to the thirtieth are known as the Council of Kadosh – the term Kadosh meaning "holy" or "consecrated". In a similar manner to the Lodge of Perfection, the first eleven of these twelve degrees are referred to as the Degrees of Areopagus – an Athenian court in ancient Greece. They are followed by the Degree Kadosh itself.

The first of the Degrees of Areopagus, the nineteenth degree, is titled Grand Pontiff. It teaches that all who believe in divine goodness and the soul are united spiritually, regardless of which particular creed they follow. Justice, truth, patience and tolerance are required to discern the difference between good and evil, between the light and the darkness, and to ensure that one fights on the right side in the constant battle between the two.

Following on from the previous degree, the twentieth degree of Master ad Vitam is a test of Masonic principles and the capacity for leadership. Justice, truth and tolerance are again the main moral lessons, on this occasion put into practice by confronting disloyalty and treason. All who work against the security and happiness of society are to be condemned.

The twenty-first degree, Patriarch Noachite, carries the important message that Freemasonry is in no way a screen behind which criminal or evil activity can be hidden. Justice being such a critical part of the Craft, it stands true that the unjust within its ranks will be even more readily identified and censured than those outside. At the same time, the degree emphasizes the vital legal principles of defending the innocent and never assuming guilt until after conviction.

Prince of Libanus is the title of the twenty-second degree. Libanus is an archaic name for Lebanon, and it was from the forests of Lebanon that the cedar trees that went into Solomon's temple were cut. This symbolism is used to hammer home that labouring for a living is inherently honourable and dignified, not a matter of shame; idleness is the true disgrace. All should work to improve conditions for those of us who labour.

In the twenty-third degree, Chief of the Tabernacle, the lesson to be taught is that it is important to work incessantly for the glory of the divine. People with faith, who hold love for their fellows, will of necessity have to make great sacrifices in order to help others. It is the only righteous way to live.

The twenty-fourth degree is titled Prince of the Tabernacle, and it explores the importance of symbolism as a universal language among the various nations of the world. It forms a route of communication for theology and fellowship between even the most disparate groups of humanity. Belief in the supreme power provides a common basis by which all people can come together in global unity, facilitated by the language of symbolism.

Every single person on Earth will have stretches in their life when they are metaphorically cast into the desert. It is inevitable. During these times, faith falters and discipline collapses as personal morale plummets. The twenty-fifth degree, Knight of the Brazen Serpent, is a reminder that this, too, shall pass. It teaches purification of the soul to remove the taint of earthly despair, so as to restore faith in the divine, in each other and in ourselves.

The twenty-sixth degree, Prince of Mercy, is a reminder to look past our own injuries and anger and treat even those who have offended against us with compassion and tenderness. Punishment must be meted out where it is deserved, but it does not have to be harshened with vengeance. It is better to treat some more gently than they deserve than to treat them more harshly.

Commander of the Temple, the twenty-seventh degree, draws on historical records of the Teutonic Knights of the House of St Mary of Jerusalem, crusaders who fought during the day, and then served as nurses and doctors at night. Their five guiding principles of temperance, generosity, chastity, honour and humility are taught.

One of the more philosophical degrees, the twenty-eighth degree, Knight of the Sun, looks at science, faith and reason. Much of its ritual material is drawn from the Kabbalah, the Jewish mystical tradition that teaches that all of creation is made up of the various emanations of ten spheres, or Sephiroth, and the 22 paths that connect them. Each sphere represents an essential principle, and the overall pattern of spheres and paths – the Tree of Life – forms a blueprint for the process of creation.

The Tree of Life is the heart of the Jewish system of mystic wisdom, known as the Kabbalah, which underpins much of the twenty-eighth degree.

The twenty-ninth degree, titled Knight of St Andrew, is the last of the Degrees of Areopagus. The lesson of this degree is that there is no such thing as a monopoly of truth. No single religion, in particular, has the absolute answer. We must remain faithful to our own convictions, but at the same time it is vital that we respect the right of others to hold different opinions. Through this, the degree aims to foster tolerance and equality.

The final degree in the Council of Kadosh is that of Knight Kadosh, the thirtieth degree. Its lesson is that tests and experiences are vital in building good character, and that all should strive practically to defend the temple of the divine within. Whether or not a person is clad in armour, he remains armed on the inside with his faith in the Supreme and his love of other people.

The thirty-first and thirty-second degrees fall under the banner of the Consistory. The thirty-first degree, Inspector Inquisitor Commander, is a reminder of the need for impartial justice, upheld with firmness but administered with mercy and forgiveness. Human nature is a weak, imperfect thing, and anyone who would judge must first look inside and judge themselves. All deserve the benefit of assuming that their intentions are innocent. While there is hope of reformation, it is vital to try to bring that hope to fruition as mercifully as possible.

The title of the thirty-second degree is Sublime Prince of the Royal Secret. Its ritual maps out the struggle between the spiritual and the animal within us all, and the victory of the spiritual. This accompanies the simultaneous victory of morality, reason and sense over the base passions and appetites. It is assumed that every Freemason is keen to serve mankind, but is frequently stuck between the demands of duty and simple self-interest. In this degree, it is acknowledged that duty often requires significant sacrifices (or more). Those who attain this degree are seen as apostles of the great principles of "Liberty, Equality and Fraternity".

The final degree of the Scottish Rite, the thirty-third degree, carries the title of Inspector General. Elevation to this degree is strictly by invitation only. Candidates are selected from the ranks of thirty-second-degree Masons who are at least 33 years of age, by ballot of the active members of a region. As there can only be 33 members of the thirty-third degree in any one region, it is an especial honour to be selected. Members who do achieve these heights are those who have made some sort of outstanding contribution in their lives to Masonry, the Scottish Rite or to the community.

Independent Orders

In addition to the two main Rites – and the satellite of appendant bodies around the York Rite – there is a number of other significant Masonic organizations that offer opportunities for further progress, study or involvement that can be thought of as neutral in terms of Rite. They all have as an absolute minimum requirement that members must be Master Masons in good standing with their Craft lodge. Some have much more stringent requirements, but all are open to both York and Scottish Rite Masons.

The Order of the Secret Monitor

One of the most highly rated independent orders is that of the Order of the Secret Monitor, also known as the Brotherhood of David and Jonathan, after the remarkably strong friendship between the two biblical figures. Its purpose is to instruct members in the importance of the virtues of friendship and fidelity. Each Conclave has four officers, known as Visiting Deacons, whose duty it is to take responsibility for one quarter of the members of the Conclave, "affording assistance and support in time of sorrow and distress". If any member is in need of any sort of genuine help or support, then the Deacon rallies the assistance of the Conclave – all strictly within the limitations of probity, legality and good faith, of course. The Order awards three degrees: Secret Monitor, Princes, and Supreme Ruler (the head of the Conclave). The Grand Conclave of the Order is based out of Mark Mason's Hall. Membership requirements vary by province, but the Order is invitational only and requires that its members are Christian. Apart from that, in some areas, simply being a Master Mason in good standing is sufficient; in others, prospective candidates are expected to be Symbolic Past Masters, Royal Arch Companions and/or members of at least one other Christian Masonic order.

The Worshipful Society

The Worshipful Society of Free Masons, Rough Masons, Wallers, Slaters, Paviors, Plaisterers and Bricklayers is an

order devoted to retaining ritual and information pertinent to the physical crafts of Masonry, information that the Speculative Lodges have moved beyond. Known as the Operatives, the order's rituals are more archaic than that of Craft Freemasonry, and contain practical instructions as well as moral lessons. Despite their archaism, the Operatives were founded only in 1913. Membership of an Assemblage is open to anyone who is in good standing as a Master Mason, a Mark Master Mason and a Royal Arch Companion. The Operatives convey seven degrees: I Degree Indentured Apprentice; II Degree Fellow of the Craft; III Degree Super-Fellow, Fitter & Marker; IV Degree Super-Fellow, Setter-Erector; V Degree Intendent, Overseer, Super Intendent & Warden; VI Degree Passed Master; and VII Degree Master Mason. Members can progress to the V Degree without further qualification, but must have been Master of both a Craft and a Mark lodge before they can reach the VI Degree and VII Degree.

The Order of the Secret Monitor celebrates the brotherly relationship between David and Jonathan – stressing the importance of friendship and fidelity – depicted here in a scene from the biblical story.

The Royal Order of Scotland

An invitational body open to Christian Masons of high achievement, the Royal Order of Scotland is administered internationally from its Grand Lodge in Edinburgh, and conveys two degrees: Heredom of Kilwinning and The Rosy Cross. Imagery for the former degree is drawn from the life of David I and looks back at the lessons and symbols of Craft Masonry; the latter is based on events of the Battle of Bannockburn and the actions of Robert the Bruce. Prospective candidates for invitation must have been Master Masons for at least five years, and have attained either the thirty-second degree in the Scottish Rite, or the York Rite rank of Order of the Temple.

The Societas Rosicruciana

A research-based order devoted to philosophy and study of the "Great Problems" of life, the nature of reality, and the "wisdom, art and literature of the ancient world", the society includes investigating topics from Gnosticism, hermeticism, the Kabbalah, alchemical research and other related matters. It currently has three independent sovereign bodies – the S. R. In Anglia, S. R. In Scotia, and S. R. In Civitatibus Foederatis – covering England, Scotland and America, respectively. Membership is restricted to Christian Master Masons. The Societas Rosicruciana has nine degrees it awards to its Fratres, namely I Degree Zelator, II Degree Theoricus, III Degree Practicus, IV Degree Philosophus, V Degree Adeptus Minor, VI Degree Adeptus Major, VII Degree Adeptus Exemptus, VIII Degree Magister and IX Degree Magus. Progression to the V Degree requires at least four years of

The Societas Rosicruciana is dedicated to philosophical study, and is open only to Master Masons in good standing.

active membership of the S. R.; the VIII Degree and IX Degree are ceremonial grades for officers of the society's High Councils, with the IX Degree in particular going only to the three superior officers – the Supreme Magus, Senior Substitute Magus and Junior Substitute Magus.

The Shriners, the Grotto and the Tall Cedars of Lebanon

In addition to these bodies, there are three organizations largely confined to North America with the very similar aims of fostering cross-jurisdictional links between individual Master Masons, having some fun and supporting a worthy charity. In each case, membership is open to all Master Masons in good standing with their lodges, regardless of constitution. The best known of these groups is the Ancient Arabic Order of the Nobles of the Mystic Shrine, also known as the Shriners. The Shriners hold regular parades and fund-raising events – and are famous for wearing red fez hats and outrageous costumes, and for "driving" in children's toy cars – to support their network of free children's hospitals around North America. The Mystic Order of Veiled Prophets of the Enchanted Realm, also known as the Grotto, have different costumes and rituals, but use much the same sort of methodology and spirit of fun fraternity as the Shriners. They work to raise money for Cerebral Palsy research. Finally, the Tall Cedars of Lebanon, named for the trees used in Solomon's temple, is another group that aims to combine fun and charity with cross-jurisdictional fellowship. Their chosen cause is muscular dystrophy and related neuromuscular disease.

There are many less-prominent bodies appendant to Freemasonry, particularly in the USA. Unfortunately this book does not have the scope to detail them all.

A Rich Tapestry

With the range of orders and other bodies available, Freemasonry is a path so varied that it is impossible to treat it in its entirety. While the exact options available vary by territory, there are well over a dozen different bodies that a member can choose to participate in, and more available by invitation, all with scores of separate degree ceremonies and hundreds of different official positions. Members can – and many do – join both the York and the Scottish Rites, and that alone is enough to fill a busy schedule, even before the social opportunities of the Craft lodge are taken into account. With all the other groups available as well, there is no shortage of material to hold one's interest. Freemasonry is a rich tapestry, and a continuing tool by which you can fight to improve yourself and the world around you – and that will always be the work of a lifetime.

Does it make you mad when you read about
Some poor, starved devil who flickered out,
Because he never had a decent chance
In the tangled meshes of circumstance?
If it makes you burn like the fires of sin,
Brother, you are fit for the ranks – fall in!

Does it make you rage when you come to learn
Of a clean-souled woman who could not earn
Enough to live, and who fought, but fell
In the cruel struggle and went to hell?

Does it make you seethe with an anger hot?
Brother we welcome you – share our lot!

Whoever has blood that will flood his face
At the sight of Beast in the Holy Place;
Whoever has rage for the tyrant's might,
For the powers that prey in the day and night;
Whoever has hate for the ravening Brute
That strips the tree of its goodly fruit;
Whoever knows wrath at the sight of pain,
Of needless sorrow and heedless gain;

Whoever knows Bitterness, shame and gall
at the thought of the trampled ones doomed to fall;
He is a brother-in-soul, we know,
With brain a-fire and soul a-glow.
By the sight of his eyes we sense our kin –
Brother, you battle with us! Fall in!

The Builder, Joseph Fort Newton, 1880–1950

The Shriners have a long history of working tirelessly on behalf of children's health, and of not taking anything else too seriously – not even a meeting with Harry Truman.

THE ARK OF THE COVENANT
SHEWING Ẏ BARRS ON Ẏ SIDE
ACCORDING TO I KINGS VIII.8
THE CHERUBIMS ABOVE ON
THE COVERING, EACH WITH
TWO WINGS WITHOUT HANDS

AND A CLOUD ABOVE BE-
TWEEN Ẏ CHERUBIMS WHICH
SEEMS TO SHINE AND, AS TO BE
IT WERE EMBRACED BY
Ẏ WINGS OF Ẏ CHERUBIMS
according to Schacous & others

2

The History of Freemasonry

Freemasonry's greatest wealth lies in the richness of its historical past, from the legendary early history, which it uses as the backdrops for its rituals and lessons, through to the social legacy that still influences us in the modern day. With almost three hundred years of well-documented notes and researches, its own modern past remains an invaluable treasury of information. More powerfully, however, Freemasonry's history anchors its goals and aspirations in a way that modern businesses and institutions lack entirely. It is fashionable now for organizations to be greedy, ruthless and short-sighted, to grab anything in sight that can be grabbed, and then squint around for more. Stress-crazed executives are forced to forget the lessons of the past and the humanity of the people around them simply to survive in the toxic corporate atmosphere. Freemasonry, in direct contrast, is completely beholden to those unfashionable, older-time concepts of justice, fairness and equity. Above all else, its history armours it against the corrosion that seems to embody modern times.

The Ark of the Covenant, the receptacle that Moses built to house the Ten Commandments, is shown resting here inside the Holy Tabernacle.

Mythic History

The core of the mythological history of Freemasonry is the story of King Solomon, son of David, who is said to have declared: "I understand the song of the birds; I am in possession of every kind of knowledge; I have been raised up to the sublime height". Certainly, Solomon's knowledge and wisdom were profound enough to have carried his reputation down the centuries – he remains the emblem of wisdom and justice right across the Western world today. He holds a special place in the heart of Freemasonry, however. As the Craft's mythological first Most Excellent Grand Master, he remains the notional law-giver, the great and wise master before all, and the object of reverential love.

Solomon was the son of King David of Israel by Bathsheba, wife of Uriah. He was born in 981 BC and, with his mother's help, came to the position of heir to David's throne. Just 20 years old when he inherited the throne from his father in 961 BC, Solomon is said to have begun his reign with a demonstration of the legendary wisdom that he possessed, successfully unknotting a legal issue of considerable difficulty.

One of Solomon's greatest goals, right from the start of his kingship, was the completion and realization of his father's dream of a mighty temple to Jehovah. It is this construction, the Temple of Solomon, that most strongly connects the king with the Craft. The erection of the temple had been a favourite dream of David's for many years, and the old king had done a lot of the groundwork. Long before his death, David had identified and counted all the workmen who were available within his kingdom. He had then examined these workers and selected those who would serve as overseers, those who would cut and shape materials and those who would be best serving as carriers of goods and burdens.

David had also drawn detailed plans of what he wanted for the temple. For many years, the Ark of the Covenant had lacked a suitable home. The Ark contained the two stone tablets that God gave to Moses, along with a jar of manna, "that they may see the bread whereby I have fed you in the wilderness", and the Rod of Aaron. The Ark itself had been made by Bezaleel and Aholiab at Moses's request. The two artisans were considered sufficiently wise to build not only the Ark, but also the

Tabernacle (the tent temple that contained it) and all its furniture. The Ark itself was 132 x 79 cm (52 x 31 in), constructed of acacia, and lined inside and out with gold. Four gold rings were set on the outside through which carrying poles could be threaded. The gilded lid of the Ark was known as the Mercy Seat, and a pair of cherubim looked at each other across it. David's dream was to build a permanent structure to replace the mobile Tabernacle as the home of God and of the Ark. Within the inner sanctum of this temple, the holy of holies, the Lord Himself would have a home on Earth. Further to this important work, he had also built up huge stockpiles of cedar, iron and brass, and set aside a vast fortune so that he could pay everyone for the goods and labour required.

When all his preparations were nearing completion, David went to consult with the prophet Nathan, to find out the auspices surrounding the project. He was dismayed to discover that although God found the piety of his intention pleasing, and judged the project free of self-aggrandizement and pride, He would not permit King David to realize his dream and fulfil the project. The prohibition was emphatic:

"Thou hast shed blood abundantly, and hast made great wars. Thou shalt not build a house unto my name, for thou hast shed much blood upon the Earth in my sight."

Not the least of which, of course, was the contrived murder of Bathsheba's husband, Uriah, by giving him suicidal military orders.

When David was close to death, he asked Solomon to swear that he would carry out the plans for the temple as soon as he was made king. He also gave his son specific instructions regarding the temple's construction, and passed to him the vast sum of money he had saved to pay for the work – said to be 10,000 talents in gold and 100,000 talents in silver. Some 40 years before, in 1000 BC, David had conquered the region of Jebus, and established a capital city there that he named Jerusalem. Mount Moriah was the holy spot where Abraham had been prepared to sacrifice his only son, Isaac, to God. It was also in the heart of Jerusalem. As the holiest of ground, it was the obvious place to build the temple.

This twelfth-century illumination tells the story of Moses calling for the Holy Tabernacle to be built, to provide a home for the Ark.

King Solomon and King Hiram

Solomon took the charge seriously. As soon as he had gained the throne he started looking at ways to put the plans into action. The sad fact, however, was that his subjects were lacking the skills required to create such an amazing temple. The Jewish people at that time were better known for their military prowess than for their engineering skills. Solomon turned for help to an old friend of his father's, Hiram, the Phoenician King of Tyre. Hiram ruled from 970 to 936 BC and had quickly established good relationships with David through a number of commercial ventures with him. Moreover, Hiram's subjects, the Tyrians and the Sidonians, were famous for their incredible skill and talent at architecture. Many of them were affiliated to a mystical pagan society of operative builders, the Fraternity of Dionysian Artificers. The fraternity actually had something of a monopoly on building, right across Asia Minor. Solomon had seen the Temple of Melgart – renowned as unmatched throughout the Eastern Mediterranean – that had been built by the Phoenician Artificers, and quickly realized that if he was going to do his father's designs justice, and get the temple erected in a reasonable amount of time and with sufficient skill to realize the vision properly, he was going to need the assistance of these foreign architects.

Accordingly, Solomon drafted a letter to Hiram of Tyre. It is recorded by the famous Jewish historian Flavius Josephus, who noted that at the time (around AD 50) the correspondence was still to be found in Jewish books of historical lore, and also in Tyrian public records:

"Thou knowest that my father would have built a temple to God, but was hindered by wars and continual expeditions, for he did not leave off to overthrow his enemies 'til he made them all subject to tribute. But I give thanks to God for the peace I at present enjoy, on which account I am at leisure and design to build a House to God, for God foretold to my father that such a House should be built by me. I desire thee to send some of thy subjects with mine to Mount Lebanon, to cut down timber, for the Sidonians are more skilful than our people in the cutting of wood. As for the wages due to the hewers of wood, I will pay whatever price thou shalt determine."

King Hiram had been a solid friend of David's and enjoyed the state of alliance that existed between the two countries, so he was inclined to extend his friendship to David's son by default, and solve a problem in the bargain. His response was enthusiastic:

"It is fitting to bless God, that He hath commended thy father's government to thee, who art a wise man and endowed with virtues. As for myself, I rejoice at the condition that thou art in, and will be subservient to thee in all that thou sendest to me about; for when, by my subjects, I have cut down many large trees of cedar and cypress wood, I will send them to sea, and will order my subjects to make floats of them, and to sail to whatsoever places of thy country thou shalt desire, and so leave them, that thy subjects may carry them to Jerusalem. But do take thou care to procure us corn for this timber, when we stand in need of, by virtue of inhabiting an island."

King Hiram was as good as his letter, and swiftly set his subjects to work. Lebanese cedar is still world-renowned today; it has a particularly good colour and solidity, and is blessed with few knots. The trees sometimes reach more than 30 m (100 ft) in height, and nowadays they are very rare. The felled wood had to be rolled down the mountainsides where it was logged, then pulled by oxen teams along 24 km (15 miles) of roads to the shore. Large rafts of logs

King Solomon receives the first instalment of timber, expert workers and materials from King Hiram of Tyre, opposite.

King Solomon, King Hiram of Tyre and Hiram Abiff are depicted here together in beautiful stained glass, designed for the Masons of Worcester, England, in memory of Provincial Grand Master Augustus Frederick Godson in Great Malvern Priory Church.

were then prepared and hauled by boat to Joppa, now known as Tel Aviv. From there, Solomon had 56 km (35 miles) of good road constructed so that the logs could be hauled to Jerusalem. All in all, it was a mammoth task.

In addition to the substantial amount of wood Hiram was providing, he cheerfully lent skilled workers to the project. The accounts record that in due course Solomon got 33,600 skilled Tyrian workers to help his own men. More importantly than men, wood or stone, however, King Hiram also sent to Solomon his most gifted architect – "a skilful man, endowed with understanding … my master craftsman, skilled to work in gold and silver, bronze and iron, stone and wood, purple and blue, fine linen and crimson, and to make any engraving and to accomplish any plan which may be given to him, with your skilful men and with the skilful men of my lord David your father." This architect was sent to supervise the construction effort, manage the Tyrian workforce, fine-tune the designs, and to lend his assistance and expertise in adding adornments and otherwise beautifying the temple. His name was Hiram Abiff. In return for all of King Hiram's help, Solomon paid a yearly basket of 2,000 tonnes of wheat, 2,000 tonnes of barley, 400,000 litres (88,000 gallons) of olive oil, and 400,000 litres (88,000 gallons) of wine.

Building the Temple

Construction on the temple began in the fourth year of Solomon's reign, in 957 BC, on a date equivalent to April 21. According to the traditions encapsulated in Masonic teaching, Solomon himself oversaw the entire work process. There were 70,000 apprentice stoneworkers in the quarries around Jerusalem performing the core of the excavation, and a further 80,000 crafts fellows tasked with cutting the rough blocks into perfect polished building stones, or ashlars. Some 30,000 further craftsmen were dedicated to cutting and preparing the Lebanese cedar wood. To keep everything running smoothly, 3,300 overseers and 500 chief overseers monitored all the work. Solomon himself managed the combined workforce, oversaw the payment of their wages, kept the workers happy and motivated, settled disputes, and generally made sure that everything went smoothly. He was assisted and advised in all matters by his two fellow Grand Masters of the Craft, King Hiram of Tyre and Hiram Abiff.

In order to make sure that everyone was treated fairly and that all workers were paid their fair dues, the workforce was divided into three large, ranked classes. These classes were based solely on the workmen's different degrees of skill and aptitude. As there was a huge number of men involved in the project – some writers, working from source, have estimated that the combined total workforce was 217,451 people – it was decided that identity rolls would prove too cumbersome. Each of the three classes of worker was taught a different set of signs and words by which they could identify themselves. When the time came to collect wages, the worker would identify himself with the signs and words that he had been taught, and so receive his fair due of payment.

The stone for the temple was cut, squared off and numbered in its quarries. The wood was cut and prepared on the outskirts of the city, where the logs were hauled in from Joppa. When they arrived at Jerusalem, these materials were further readied for use, with a variety of finishing touches being put in place. The famous bronzed pillars of the temple had to be prepared almost 100 km (60 miles) northeast of Jerusalem, where the copper mines were located. Since each was some 9 m (30 ft) high and 5 m (20 ft) in diameter, transporting them back to Jerusalem must have been a profound task. Each pillar was crowned with a headpiece some 2.25 m

(7½ ft) high, in the shape of lilies. The pillars were cast from brass and left hollow so that they could store ancient records and valuable writings of the Jewish peoples. The left-hand pillar represented the land of Judah, while the right-hand one represented Israel. When the two were set in place in the temple and united by the Lintel of Jehovah, which ran between them, they were said to represent stability.

The materials were prepared for their final placing before being conveyed to the Temple Mount. On arrival, they were put in place and, where necessary, fixed with wooden mauls, so that: "There was neither hammer nor axe nor any tool of iron heard in the House while it was in building". According to tradition, the Lord himself took an active hand in the construction – for the whole time that the building was in progress, God made sure that the rains never fell during the day, so as to avoid disturbing the workers from their labours. The temple was constructed on an east–west orientation, and surrounded by a high wall of stone and timber. Its

outer walls were said to reach some 152 x 229 m (500 x 750 ft). These held the inner court, which was said to reach 64 m (209 ft) from each wall of the temple proper to the outer wall.

Of the three Grand Masters, King Solomon was in charge of managing the project and the design specifics; King Hiram of Tyre maintained responsibility for supply and other logistical matters; and Hiram Abiff was the superintendent of building, both of the construction effort and the growing temple itself. The junior stations were given to other eminent builders and artists. According to the internal mythology of Freemasonry, the most important of these other artisans were Adoniram and Tito Zadok.

Adoniram was Hiram Abiff's brother-in-law, and he was granted the title of inspector. He seems to have been Abiff's second-in-command, and therefore worthy of much respect. During the first stages of organization in Jerusalem he was in charge of the workmen. After Hiram Abiff's arrival, Adoniram was sent to oversee and inspect the works on Mount Lebanon, where several thousand Tyrian crafters and Jewish levies were helping to prepare the wood for transport.

Tito Zadok, Prince of the Harodim, was the high priest. He was put in charge of the 300 architects who had been chosen to oversee the quartermastering of the raw materials. He also oversaw the school of architecture that Solomon had founded for the workmen. His idea was that while the workmen laboured on building the temple, they would also be able to obtain more advanced instruction from masters of the craft. That way, their skills would improve considerably as the temple progressed, and some measure of Tyre's expertise would be passed to Jerusalem.

Another of Solomon's innovations was to divide the Jewish workmen into 12 groups, each group consisting solely of the men of one of the 12 tribes. A well-known knight from the tribe was placed in charge of the group. Every evening, the 12 knights were charged with reporting directly to Solomon, to inform him how much

The Holy Tabernacle surrounded by a massive tent encampment is shown opposite. Note the altar and bowl out in front of the holy of holies.

The pillars on this Scottish Rite Masonic Apron, left, represent the two mighty pillars that stood at the entrance to Solomon's temple.

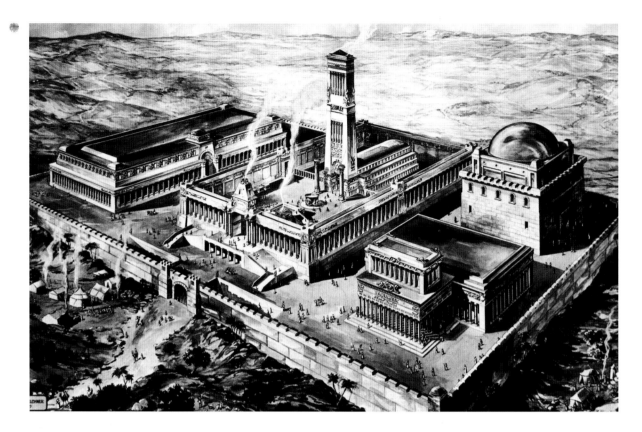

In this updated version of John W. Kelchner's 1913 reconstruction of King Solomon's temple, Abiff's Molten Sea can be seen in front of the pillars guarding the inner sanctum.

A 1705 Dutch interpretation of the final design of Solomon's temple – this one is interestingly reminiscent of a Victorian city block.

work their tribe had carried out that day. The good-natured competition that this policy engendered helped to ensure that each man worked to the best of his capacity. In every aspect of the construction effort, Solomon turned his insight and wisdom into ways to improve and perfect. Those with the quickest minds and deepest loyalties, those whose enthusiasm and fidelity were inspirational to all around them, the most exceptional of the workers were all gathered up and anointed as masters. They were set to their strengths, to instruct or oversee or take care of fine work as best fitted their natures. Those who were not so blessed were yet enthused by the possibilities of promotion and increased reward, available to all who increased their skills through practice and instruction at the school, and who performed their tasks well and diligently.

The Molten Sea and Jesus' Cradle

In the southeast corner, Hiram Abiff cunningly fashioned a small wonder called the Molten Sea. It was a huge, circular, cast-bronze bowl a little short of 2.4 m (8 ft) in height and around 4.5 m (15 ft) in diameter, capable of holding 45,000 litres (10,000 gallons) of water. All around the rim were rows of gourds, cast as part of the whole piece, and the entire structure was supported by a dozen bronze bulls, clustered in groups of three. It provided the high priests of the temple with a sacred lake to cleanse themselves. An ornate bronze altar sat in front of the left-hand pillar, on four stepped, stone plinths, each smaller than the last. Ten beautifully worked bronze carts sat around the altar, decorated with angels, palm trees, bulls and lions, and carrying basins of water in which sacrificial animals could be cleansed.

The temple itself is thought to have been around 38 m long, 20 m wide and 12 m high (125 x 65 x 40 ft). Three levels of "side chambers" were in place all around the outside of the temple, for a total of 90 rooms, 30 on each storey. The lowest level was accessed from the south side of the temple, with a stairway in the southeast corner winding up to the middle level, and a further staircase going from that level to the topmost one. Neither the side chambers nor their level walkways gave any access to the inside of the temple. Entry to the temple was via a wide porch and entrance hall in the front of the building, which the great pillars of bronze flanked. It is assumed that the temple itself followed the common Phoenician design, with an outer hallway, a central open space and then the curtained-off holy of holies, the sanctum sanctorum. The large open space, the sanctuary, was lit by small windows, and lavishly decorated and furnished with all the finest items that the genius of Hiram Abiff could conjure. The sanctuary's main altar was 2.25 m (7½ ft) square and 1.4 m (4½ ft) high, made of acacia covered with gold. Four horns stuck up from the four corners. Directly behind it, a pair of gorgeous double doors led to the stairs that ran up to the curtained holy of holies, a space that was a perfect 9 m (30 ft) cube, raised 3 m (10 ft) off the floor and coated on all surfaces with beaten and polished gold.

Once all the organizational structures and architectural plans were set and work was underway, King Solomon made a mighty discovery in the temple foundations. Work had uncovered a vault, buried deep under ground. Solomon discovered further vaults beneath it and, in the lowest vault of all, he found a stone cube that bore a triangular plate of agate, gold and precious stones. The Tetragrammaton, the true name of God, was inscribed on the plate. This was the foundation stone that the prophet Enoch had constructed and consecrated according to God's orders. Once a year only, Enoch (and after him, his inheritor according to his line) was allowed to uncover the series of vaults and descend to the presence of the foundation stone, on which he offered suitable sacrifices to the glory of God. After the great flood, however, the stone was lost to the world for ages, and all knowledge of its location passed away.

Recognizing the sanctity and importance of his discovery, Solomon removed the stone of foundation and gave it a new home in the temple's holy of holies, the inner sanctum where only the high priest would be permitted, and then only on the Day of Atonement. There he set it in the west, where it could act as a pedestal for the Ark of the Covenant in due course, and laid Aaron's rod and a pot of manna in front of it. Later, after the temple's completion, Solomon had the stone moved again to an even more secure location, so that it would be undisturbed even if the temple itself should be destroyed.

And so work progressed for seven years, until the temple was nearly complete. At that point, Masonic legend tells us, work was horribly derailed by the cruel murder of Solomon's chief advisor, the architect Hiram Abiff. After a period of searching, Abiff's body was discovered. Solomon, nearly beside himself with grief and anger at the loss of his friend, still managed to cling on to his wits and wisdom. With the aid of a carefully thought-out and well-executed plan, he apprehended the murderers and punished them as they deserved.

Once the matter of the murder was dealt with and put behind, Solomon did the best he could to see that Hiram Abiff's work would be continued to the completion of the temple. He appointed several new officers at new ranks and degrees, and divided Hiram Abiff's labours among them. Architectural work was divided among several skilled men of suitable ability, architects who had been under the care and instruction of Tito Zadok. They were labelled intendants of the building. The task of administration regarding matters of justice was passed to another group of dedicated, unimpeachable men, called provosts and judges. With the aid of all these loyal masters, Solomon was able to patch the void left by Hiram Abiff and keep progress running on the construction until its completion.

The temple was finally completed late in the year 960 BC, a little more than seven years from when the project was started. As soon as it was complete, Solomon was determined to honour properly the glorious edifice so that it would be fit to be the house of God. He summoned the various heads of the tribes of Israel and all the other elders and chiefs and hierarchs, and ordered that the Ark of the Covenant should be retrieved from the Holy Tabernacle in Zion, where David had left it until a more fitting place could be found. The Levites fetched it and delivered it to the priests of the temple. On the Day of Atonement, the Ark was then placed in the holy of holies on the stone of foundation, as the culmination of a series of long and joyous ceremonies. When the Ark was safely in place, God filled the temple with a cloud of glory as a sign that he had taken up residence, and no other could enter the temple. Over the seven days that followed, Solomon led prayers of dedication and sanctification, and sacrificed 22,000 cattle and 120,000 sheep.

The First Masons

The completion of the temple marks the completed organization of Freemasonry. The Tyrian architects, who possessed great skill at architecture, gained the light of Solomon's wisdom and piety; the Jewish workers, whose piety was unquestioned, gained the cunning workmanship of their Tyrian brothers. Solomon's wisdom was so great that his moral code and teachings were embodied within every detail of his system for the organization of Masonry, encoded in symbol and sign.

Solomon's temple stood out over Jerusalem for almost 400 years until it was destroyed by King Nebuchadnezzar of Babylon in 586 BC. Nearly 50 years later, in 538 BC, King Cyrus of Persia captured Babylon and released

the Hebrews, who had been enslaved in Babylon. They then returned to Jerusalem to rebuild the temple under the direction of Zerubbabel (see also pages 38–40). This reconstruction was finally finished in 515 BC.

Centuries later, in 164 BC, Judah Maccabee captured Jerusalem and performed a great deal of restoration work on the temple, but the Romans under their great general Pompey took the city in 63 BC, and it was then extensively plundered in 54 BC by the then Roman consul, Crassus. Herod took the city in 37 BC, and some time around 20 BC once again started rebuilding it. Work continued until AD 64. However, almost no sooner had the temple been completed once more than the Romans sacked Jerusalem and destroyed it again, effectively ending its history. Only a fragment of the

As the last fragment of God's House on Earth (the last remaining structure of Solomon's temple), the Wailing Wall is the holiest site in Christendom today.

temple's outer wall still stands today – now the Wailing Wall – and it is one of the world's most important pilgrimage destinations.

Solomon's reign lasted 40 years, and when he died the glory and power of the Hebrew empire died with him, but the legacy of his teaching and wisdom remained. These precepts have survived down the long centuries, worked within the Mason's craft, to come down finally to us today, their teaching power intact … or so the legends say, anyway.

Esoteric History

To the bemusement of many Freemasons, there seem to be persistent rumours that Masonry is the inheritor and guardian of all sorts of profound occult secrets. These range from theoretic hordes of Templar gold and long-lost snippets of arcane wisdom right up to world-shattering relics, such as the Holy Grail, the Ark of the Covenant and the Spear of Longinus, the weapon used to pierce Christ's side while he hung on the cross. Rumours of this type normally seem to assume that there is some sort of secret inner council that governs the whole of Freemasonry, although it should be clear from the previous chapter that such a thing would be quite impossible. However persistent the rumours and hearsay get, though, there is no denying that Freemasonry had to have acquired (or synthesized) its spiritual symbolism and moral lessons from somewhere. It is likely that we'll never know the real early history of Freemasonry's spiritual development, but there are plenty of different theories.

The Teaching Tradition

Freemasonry's own body of internal legends suggests that the spiritual teachings of the craft are derived directly from Solomon's own wisdom, preserved through guilds and societies of operative (in other words, professional) stonemasons down through the ages. There is certainly no denying that Freemasonry owes a considerable debt to the operative mason's guilds of the Middle Ages, particularly in Scotland. The structure of meeting as a lodge can certainly be traced back to the operative guilds, as can certain symbolic elements of the Craft.

This is backed up with clear documentary evidence – the oldest known active lodge in Freemasonry is the lodge of Edinburgh Mary's Chapel, now under the Grand Lodge of Scotland, which possesses continuous written records going back to the year 1599, more than a century and a quarter before the official birth of modern Freemasonry. Other lodges have origins that are likely to stretch back at least as far, but the documentary evidence is no longer available – Mother Kilwinning Lodge, for example, also now under the Grand Lodge of Scotland. From the evidence that these Lodges of Time Immemorial (as they are known) can provide, we can be confident that modern Masonry isn't just a copy of the old stone guilds – it's a direct transmission.

Because we can be confident of this, it is tempting to think that the spiritual component of Freemasonry could have been transmitted along the same route, out of the depths of mythic history. The legend inside Freemasonry is that after the building of Solomon's temple, the Dionysian Artificers of Tyre (and Phoenicia in general) absorbed the King's wisdom and piety into a coherent structure. That structure became a system of moral improvement that was strengthened and honed over the centuries, until it was passed on to Pythagoras and his network of students and schools. The Pythagorean tradition harboured this wisdom until it was absorbed into the Roman Collegia (guilds), which chiefly taught actual architectural skills.

When Rome fell and the barbarians destroyed the Collegia, we know that a small number of architectural guilds survived in Lombardy, in northern Italy, near Lake Como. These architects – known as the Comacine Masters, after the lake – were the last bastion of the Collegia, and the inheritors of the Pythagorean wisdom. They flourished through the Dark Ages, possibly sending Masons to England with St Augustine around AD 600. They continued on long past this, however, eventually releasing certain ancient techniques retained from the Dionysians, which were used on Noah's Ark. These became the inspiration for the gothic architectural movement. The secrets of Masonry thus passed from the Comacine guilds to the cathedral builders of the twelfth century. The work of these cathedral architects duly attracted interest and would-be students, and the medieval stonemason's guilds accreted around them to pass Solomon's light on to modern Freemasonry.

There is a number of very significant problems with this myth, however. Perhaps the greatest is that there is no shred of evidence anywhere to suggest the transmission of any spiritual or mystical tradition along the chain of architectural knowledge. It is possible that Pythagoras acquired some spiritual teachings from the Dionysians, but very unlikely that this was then passed on in the Collegia to the Comacines. We also don't really know how influential the Comacines were by the end of the Dark Ages, and there's absolutely no evidence that

St Augustine, shown here surrounded by demons trying
unsuccessfully to distract him from creating his masterpiece,
The City of God.

An illustration of the first crusade by Gustave Doré, in which a group of knights set out to the Holy Land. This event paved the way for the creation of the Knights Templar and other holy orders.

gothic architecture was anything other than a new innovation. It seems probable that any spiritual learning the cathedral builders acquired could easily have come from their continued exposure to eloquent, high-ranking clergy as they built the cathedrals.

Additionally, symbolic Masonry itself poses some questions for the legend. The third craft degree of Master Mason is rich with symbolism, but little of it is appropriate to operative stonemasonry or architecture. Why would such a ritual have survived without picking up a more operative flavour? Even assuming it just did, however, the symbolic teaching tools of the first degree are highly inconsistent with the trade tools that would have been given to a rank beginner – a major block to assuming the degrees are taken straight from any operative teaching. Such an incongruity would not have

A portrait of Jacques de Molay, the ill-fated last Grand Master of the Knights Templar, who was executed in 1314.

survived 3,000 years of transmission from operative mason to operative mason; it would have been corrected to make more sense. The myth of direct operative transmission from Solomon is just that – a myth.

The Poor Knights of Christ and the Temple of Solomon

The Knights Templar have been a source of endless fascination and inspiration for the Western mystery tradition for as long as it has existed. Founded in 1118 by Sir Yves de Faillon to protect pilgrims travelling from Europe to the Holy Land after the first crusade, the Knights Templar were initially based on Mount Moriah itself. They took over the el-Aqsa Mosque, which the crusaders called the Temple of Solomon because of its position on the ruins of the old temple. The Templars enlarged the mosque and co-opted the vaults beneath it as stables. They grew quickly, gaining wealth and prestige.

Over time they moved their emphasis back to Europe and became extremely rich and powerful (as bankers, effectively), until they were finally suppressed in 1307 by Philip, King of France with the assistance of Pope Clement V. Many Templars fled the suppression, and their treasures vanished with them. In Portugal, they renamed themselves the Order of Christ, and helped the country become a naval power. In Spain, they merged quietly into the Order of Montessa. In Scotland, the king had already been excommunicated by the Pope, and so blithely ignored the order of suppression. The English king dragged his heels over it for years as well. Elsewhere, when the suppression held, Templar assets went to the Knights Hospitaller, and many of the surviving Templar members transferred, too.

Meanwhile, those Templars who were captured were tortured into confessing all manner of occult and satanic crimes. They were accused of worshipping a talking head named Baphomet, which they had found deep in Mount Moriah – and of many other things besides, including homosexual activity, spitting on the cross, and all the usual charges levied against would-be heretics. The Grand Master, Jacques de Molay, was eventually executed late in 1314. As he burned, he cursed King Philip and Pope Clement to death before a year was out – Clement lasted just a month before dying, and Philip only six months further. The Catholic Church has long held the position that the Templars were innocent, and that the Pope had been manipulated into suppressing them. Evidence to this effect was found in 2001 in the Vatican's secret archives, when a researcher uncovered a document showing that Clement secretly pardoned the Templars some months before de Molay's execution.

During their period of growth, it is suggested that the Templars may have come into contact with ancient mystery sects and orders that had been founded by Tyrian and Hebrew Masons who elected to remain in Jerusalem and the vicinity after the construction of Solomon's temple. These sects may have preserved all manner of lore regarding the temple, including the story of the murder of Hiram Abiff, which does not appear in any written record. The Templars could then have learned the ancient secrets from these sects, in Jerusalem or in Syria. Certainly, as time passed the order became

This painting shows a Templar in discussion with Pope Clement and King Phillip before the society was forcibly disbanded.

much more ritualized and secretive than it had been, which might indicate a transition to a structure based on a hidden sect.

During the height of their power in Europe, the Templars built a huge number of preceptories, temples, churches and other buildings. If they had learned ancient secret traditions related to stonemasonry and architecture, they could very easily have passed these on to the architects they were working with in the construction of their properties. More directly, it is thought that a substantial number of European Templars escaped the initial suppression by fleeing to England, and from there up to Scotland, where they were never suppressed at all. They then pass out of official history, but it has been claimed that they continued their order. In time, certain segments could have migrated from the Templar structure to take symbolic positions in the medieval stone guilds. This would provide a direct line of transmission to modern Freemasonry – maybe even a conduit by which Freemasonry could be seen as the direct child of the Templar's spiritual teachings.

It's an interesting theory, and one that appeals to romantics and mystics alike – what secrets might the Templar mystics have carried out of long-hidden vaults on Mount Moriah, and passed down the centuries to the earliest Scots Masons? Sadly, there isn't a shred of hard evidence to support any of it. We don't even know whether any French Masons escaped the purge – some historians claim all were caught, others that the order was forewarned, and just a few remained as sacrificial lambs – and secrets or treasures could have ended up almost anywhere. Some fourteenth- and fifteenth-century graves in Scotland do seem to suggest a Templar link, but there's no way to be certain. Also, if the Templars did survive, why would they have diluted their secrets by passing them to Scots stonemasons, or even to Freemasons?

The Rosicrucian Order

According to the mainstream legend, the mythic founder of the Rosicrucian Order was Christian Rosenkreuz, a German who was born in 1378 and purportedly travelled throughout the Holy Land studying occult wisdom under a variety of Eastern and Middle Eastern masters. He supposedly founded the order in 1407, and kept it small

Once the Templars were
declared heretics, Philip
the Fair arrested as many
of them as he could get
his hands on.

Many Templars, convicted
of witchcraft, blasphemy
and heresy, ended up
being burned at the stake.

– no more than eight members. When he died in 1484, at the age of 106, the order made itself totally secret, at Rosenkreuz's request, for a further 120 years. It was then reborn in 1614, when a series of enigmatic pamphlets announced its presence to a captivated Europe.

A lesser-known variant of the legend states that the Rosicrucian Order was formed by an Alexandrian sage named Ormus in AD 46. The apostle Mark converted Ormus and his followers to Christianity, and the resulting fusion of ancient Egyptian magical lore and Christian teachings became the bedrock of the order. It continued underground for 1,400 years before Christian Rosenkreuz – the Grand Master at the time – let it enter the history books.

Factual knowledge of the Rosicrucian movement begins in 1614, with the anonymous publication Europe-wide of a document known as the *Fama Fraternitatis Rosae Crucis*. This was followed in 1615 by the *Confessio Fraternitatis*, and finally in 1616 by *The Chymical Wedding of Christian Rosenkreuz*. The documents were highly mystical and allegorical, hinting at all manner of occult secrets that an adept might discern. They encouraged further research into their mysteries, and carried a general tone of moral improvement and religious reformation. The leaflets caused a huge amount of excitement and speculation, and provoked a barrage of similar material.

A number of mystic, hermetic and alchemic authors identified themselves as Rosicrucians, but there is no actual evidence to suggest an active order – it appears as if they were working in isolation, taking advantage of an exciting new label compatible with their personal beliefs. In fact, the whole thing almost certainly started with the author of the three leaflets, and may well have been a whimsy concocted by a theologian named Johann Valentin Andrea. If so, the joke somewhat backfired,

A page from *The Chymical Wedding of Christian Rosenkreuz*. The manuscripts are still in existence, preserved for study in major library collections.

This promotional poster by Albinet, for the Third Salon on April 7, 1894, depicts Christian Rosenkreuz and an anonymous Templar in front of the Red Grail.

as it provoked a lot of thought, debate and research. Famous historical Rosicrucians include Leonardo da Vinci, Isaac Newton, Rene Descartes, alchemist Ramon Lull, Ludwig van Beethoven and the hermetic philosopher Paracelsus.

The interest, from a Masonic point of view, lies in Rosenkreuz's experiences in the Holy Land. While studying with the secret masters he found there, it is argued that he could have learned the secrets of Solomon's wisdom and the legends of the temple from the surviving remnants of the Tyrian masters and their descendants. This wisdom then travelled back with him to Europe and became part of the Rosicrucian teachings when he founded the order. After the order went public in 1614, there was a great deal of interest. One of the learned Rosicrucians who had been taught the secrets of Solomon's wisdom became involved with the nascent Masonic organizations, and passed the mysteries on to

It is widely thought possible that theological scholar Johann Valentin Andrea, above, created the Rosicrucian pamphlets as a sly, satirical joke.

his brethren. From there, they developed into what would become modern Freemasonry.

It is certain that some of the earliest members of Symbolic (in other words, non-operative) Masonry were also highly interested in Rosicrucianism – such as Elias Ashmole, who was initiated in 1640 – and that others who undoubtedly influenced its development, such as the philosopher Robert Fludd, were also of a Rosicrucian bent. The progressive, moral, symbolic nature of the Rosicrucian message could certainly have been an influence on the development of Freemasonry. However, it only serves as a vehicle for the transmission of the Solomonic material if Rosenkreuz was a real figure – and that seems very unlikely.

The Kabbalah

The mystic tradition of the Jewish religion, the Kabbalah, claims to offer insight into the nature of the divine and the process of creation. It has been claimed that it can provide a way for mankind to begin to apprehend the ineffable nature of God himself – or at least to take a person as far in that direction as the human mind is capable of comprehending. According to this theory, Freemasonry is a reworking of Kabbalistic principles, a veiled allegory to the mystic path of Judaism.

The Kabbalah has been a matter of philosophical and religious thought and research by orthodox Judaism for almost 2,000 years, but it wasn't until the sixteenth century that it really gained popularity in Western mystic thought. The advent of publishing transformed what had been a firmly oral tradition passed from master to student into a readily accessible, broadly outlined set of mystical ideas. In particular, a book entitled the *Zohar* (or Book of Splendour) really provided the Kabbalah with the strong foundation it needed to gain widespread recognition. This firmed the subject in Jewish thought as well, so that the *Zohar*'s precepts have become standard teachings.

The Kabbalah states that all creation is divided into four worlds, representing descending levels of awareness: the divine, the intellectual, the emotional and the instinctual. These worlds are all made up, effectively, of light emanating from 10 different spheres (Sephiroth), which is channelled down a system of 22 paths (Nativoth) which link them. In this way, the unbearable light of

God's radiance in the first sphere takes form and substance until the tenth sphere brings it into being. Curiously, there are some interesting parallels between Kabbalistic theories of manifestation and the current cutting edge of quantum mechanics theory.

The spheres and paths together are arranged into a pattern called the Tree of Life, or Otz Chi'im. Every facet of reality is made up of the emanations of these spheres, as patterned and modulated by the paths, and birthed through the final sphere. Just as each of the four worlds is a descent from the one above it, so too each has a Tree of Life of its own, with its final sphere forming the first sphere of the next level down.

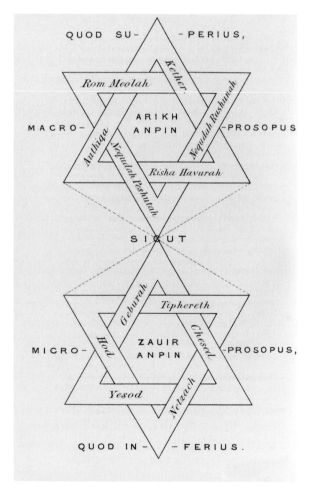

This illustration from the *Zohar* illustrates the mystic principle that states: As Above, So Below – that Earth reflects Heaven.

The philosophical implication is clear: to reach a level of awareness, one has to master and transcend the level beneath it. Beasts are stuck on the instinctual level, while humans transcend that awareness as they develop speech. Some remain mired in the emotional, while others are able to move past that level to the intellectual, mastering themselves. According to Kabbalistic philosophy, the ultimate goal of all humans – of all energy – is to perfect the emotional and intellectual, and transcend them, being reborn into the divine and seeking understanding with the light.

According to this theory, the mystical and spiritual content of Freemasonry is derived largely from Kabbalistic principles. The Kabbalistic path aims to provide a route for the perfection of the soul and the attainment of grace; it can be said that so, too, does Freemasonry. The three degrees of Freemasonry can be said to parallel the three conscious worlds of the Kabbalah. The rituals of the first degree do deal with ethical (and, therefore, emotive) issues, while the second degree discusses intellectual issues, and the third degree symbolizes the process of death and rebirth into spiritual awareness. Furthermore, 10 Sephiroth and 22 Nativoth total 32 elements – the same as the progressively attainable grades of the Scottish Rite – while the four worlds can also correspond to the four chief bodies of the York Rite. Similar parallels in symbolism exist throughout every level of detail if you look hard enough; even the three Greater Lights of the lodge can be seen as the three "Veils" of light above the Tree of Life that are said to prevent God's radiance from blasting creation: the Ain ("Nothing"), the Ain Soph ("Without Limit") and the Ain Soph Aur ("Limitless Light").

In the end, though, the human mind is specifically geared to noticing patterns, finding equivalences and drawing parallels. It's the way that our minds order reality, so that we can experience it. If you look hard enough, you can find a frightening wealth of parallels between any two complex systems. It's particularly true for the Kabbalah, which is highly flexible. Kabbalists say that this is because all things that are contain the Tree of Life within them; be that as it may, that remains a religious statement rather than a causal description. When all is said and done, although there are certainly

strong Kabbalistic overtones to some degrees, there
is no particular reason to believe that all of modern
Freemasonry is a Kabbalistic retelling.

Esoteric Conclusions

There may well be Kabbalistic derivations in Masonry.
Certainly the Kabbalistic goal of perfecting the self
through rebirth into higher awareness sits very nicely
with the goals of Freemasonry as a system. There are
undeniably large swathes of very powerful scriptural
material. In assorted places across Masonry, parallels
can be drawn with thought and symbolism of all the
major religions. Both Templar and Rosicrucian imagery
certainly have a strong place in the Masonic orders.
There can be no doubt that Freemasonry contains
symbols and icons drawn from all manner of traditions
and settings. Does this necessarily mean that it is the
inheritor of any one of them?

Surely, the clearest conclusion of all this mystic
evidence is that the moral and spiritual aspects of
Freemasonry were compiled by flexible, broadly read
philosophers of nature and morality. Their knowledge of
psychology and spirituality must have been profound,
and the implication is that they had studied the lessons
of all the great teachers, paying no heed to the religions
and regions involved. Freemasonry takes specific pains
to be inclusive to all religions, after all. The effort and
wisdom required to look across all these different
branches of spiritual learning and assemble from them a
coherent, self-contained and, above all, elegant system of
moral self-improvement must have been immense. To
then hang these teachings inside the existing framework
of the stonemason's guilds – giving it the strong initial
base it required to survive – was a stroke of brilliance.

Given the evidence of the records that remain, the
modern system must have been under development as
the operative stone mason guilds started admitting
speculative members, and was certainly seen through to
completion by the time the third degree was finalized,
sometime around 1725. By drawing on so many rich and
powerful sources, the creators of Freemasonry made sure
that their system would be vibrant, elegant and enduring
… but they also made it easy to find evidence for just
about any conspiracy or pattern you care to search for.

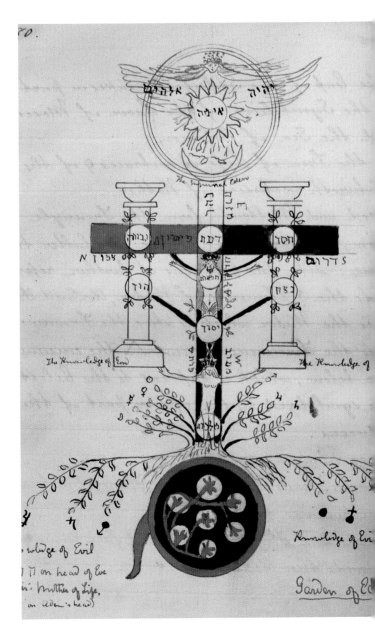

**The left- and right-hand "pillars" of the Tree of Life correspond
closely to the pillars that stood outside Solomon's temple.**

Known History

The earliest traces of Masonic practice are found in a pair of documents from the early Middle Ages, the Regius manuscript and the Cooke manuscript, dated around 1390 and 1450 respectively. The Regius poem was probably written by a priest. It discusses King Athelstan's formation of an early stonemason's guild in York during the tenth century, and includes a number of ethical and behavioural commandments that echo some of modern Freemasonry's precepts. The Cooke manuscript, on the other hand, was written by a Mason, and deals almost entirely with speculative (rather than operative) matters. It was obviously inspirational for the founders of modern Masonry, as it includes references to critical Masonic symbolism and thought, including the building of Solomon's temple, and the seven liberal arts and sciences. An operative guild of Masons in London, the Company of Free Masons, is recorded as being granted a Coat of Arms in 1473. Like the other Livery Societies of London, it would have been a cooperative trade guild.

Early Masonic history really takes off with the Schaw Statutes, dated 1598 and 1599. William Schaw was the Master of Works and Warden General for King James VI of Scotland, a post he had held since 1583. The first two statutes formalized the duties that lodge members were required to perform, barred members from working with unqualified Masons, and listed the penalties for sub-standard or unprofessional work. More significantly, the second of the two statutes contained subtle hints regarding a body of spiritual knowledge, and it required lodges to test members' skills of memorization. It also specified that all lodges were to keep written records, and confirmed that Lodge Kilwinning was active at the time.

Schaw's requirement that lodges keep minutes heralded the start of available Masonic data. The earliest record of an initiation anywhere is the inclusion of Laird Boswell of Auchenleck in the Edinburgh Mary's Chapel Lodge, on June 8, 1600. Boswell, as nobility, was most certainly not a stone-worker, so his initiation is often heralded as the first known speculative raising.

First Initiates

In England, the earliest recorded initiation is that of Sir Robert Moray (1641) in a lodge of Masons attached to a Scottish regiment located in Newcastle upon Tyne. However, the Worshipful Company of Freemasons of London, the Livery company, has records dating back to 1621 that indicate its members were divided into "operative" and "accepted" categories. Incidentally, the first recorded initiation of an American is thought to be the Governor of Massachusetts, Jonathan Belcher, in 1704, while the first recorded initiation performed in Australia – of a captain in the New South Wales Corps, Anthony Kemp – was performed aboard a French boat in Sydney Harbour, and dates to 1802.

In 1646, a famous writer, historian and philosopher named Elias Ashmole was initiated into Freemasonry. Ashmole was a member of the Invisible College, a scientific and philosophical society made up of the greatest thinkers of the day. Fellows of the College included Isaac Newton, Christopher Wren, Francis Bacon, Robert Boyle, Dr John Wilkins and the aforementioned Sir Robert Moray. The College would eventually win a royal charter from Charles II in 1662 and become the famous Royal Society – many of its members being Masons – but before that time membership would have been risky at best. Ashmole also mentions attending a lodge meeting in 1682, but apart from these sketchy notes in his diaries, little Masonic information remains from the seventeenth century in England.

As Samuel Pepys' diaries clearly recall, the times were extremely volatile, and anything that threatened established thinking or smacked of conspiracy was apt to cause serious, even fatal trouble. It was still possible to get burned at the stake for heresy or witchcraft. Francis Bacon's works had been banned by the Catholic Church and the Inquisition was itching to get hold of him; Galileo, likewise, was anathema for his insistence that the Earth rotated around the Sun. It is little surprise then that the Invisible College was secretive, and that its

An entry ticket for a Masonic assembly in Glasgow, Scotland, 1885, is shown above – note the pillars bordering the ticket.

The engraving, left, by T. Higham, depicts Freemasons from the Lodge of St James holding a procession in Tarbolton, Scotland, around the turn of the nineteenth century. It illustrates one of Robert Burns's poems.

Elias Ashmole's diaries remain some of the earliest surviving evidence of the scope of early modern Freemasonry.

members were attracted to Freemasonry. It is entirely possible that the idea of promulgating a moral and spiritual code within the structure of an operative stone-workers' guild dates from this time. By hiding among the operative stonemasons, the thinkers and intellectual liberals could significantly reduce the danger they were in, giving themselves a very plausible route of denial. The symbolism of stonemasonry would have added a further layer of security. What better historical symbol for a group of natural philosophers than King Solomon, the wisest figure in all of history? Nobody really knows whether speculative Freemasonry in England just copied the look and feel of the Scottish operative Masonic lodges, or whether it blended with genuine operative groups within its own borders and took them over. It doesn't really matter all that much, though; the end result – and the protective camouflage – was much the same.

Modern Masonry

It is generally accepted that modern Masonic history began on June 24, 1717, when four lodges in London – the lodge of the Rummer and Grapes Tavern in Westminster, the lodge of the Apple Tree Tavern on Charles Street, the lodge of the Goose & Gridiron in St Paul's Churchyard and the lodge of the Crown Ale House near Drury Street – decided to come together and form a supervisory body, the Premier Grand Lodge of London. Their inaugural meeting was at the Goose & Gridiron. The four lodges – with a combined membership of 115 Masons, two-thirds of whom belonged to the Rummer and Grapes – elected a set of Grand Officers, and a first Grand Master, Anthony Sayer. Three of the four lodges are still active: the Goose & Gridiron is now known as Antiquity Lodge #2, the Rummer and Grapes is now Royal Somerset House and Inverness Lodge #4, and the Apple Tree is now Lodge Fortitude and Old Cumberland #12, all constituted under UGLE.

The new Grand Lodge spread its influence very swiftly. By 1721, it had restyled itself the Premier Grand Lodge of England, and had more than 50 lodges from London and the surrounding area under its wing. At its fourth anniversary meeting, the Duke of Montague was elected as Grand Master, which greatly increased the

This eighteenth-century engraving shows the constitutions of Freemasonry being passed along by Dr James Anderson, while Heaven watches on approvingly.

Craft's prestige and brought a lot of publicity. At the same time, the Grand Lodge first adopted its policy that all regular lodges were required to obtain a charter from the Grand Lodge. Two years later, in 1723, Dr James Anderson – son of a prominent Scottish Past Master – produced a book of Constitutions for the Grand Lodge, which laid down rules, regulations, codes and procedures, and is still substantially unchanged today.

There has been a lot of speculation regarding the Grand Lodge's meteoric success. Why, in particular, should so many lodges enthusiastically let a small group of Masons from central London take power over them, dictate behaviour and conditions, and even charge them dues for the privilege? One possible answer has been suggested by authors Michael Baigent and Richard Leigh. In a follow-up to their best-selling *The Holy Blood and the Holy Grail* (reworked as a story by Dan Brown in his smash hit *The Da Vinci Code*), the authors turn their attentions to the Templars, the Scots and the Freemasons.

The book, entitled *The Temple and the Lodge*, suggests that the main cause for the spread of Grand Lodge was the failed Jacobite revolution of 1715 against the new English royal dynasty of Hanover. Freemasonry's Scottish roots are strong, and the aftermath of the Jacobite attempt did not entirely die until 1717.

At that time, the authors suggest, there may have been much very genuine fear that Freemasonry would be seen as a seditious, pro-Jacobite conspiracy – which is exactly what it was in France, where the Jacobites had fled to, and remained such for years. Desperate to establish neutrality, the Grand Lodge gave a chance for lodges to espouse specifically anti-political, anti-religious and anti-revolutionary policies, and to organize into a body that would be seen to enforce good behaviour and loyalty. At the same time, it allowed the lodges to distance themselves from their Scottish past – a Premier Grand Lodge of England, taking the coat of arms of the Livery Society of London Freemasons, immediately established itself as a thoroughly London-centred movement with centuries of local history behind it.

Seen from that point of view, the establishment of the Grand Lodge would not have been an imposition or tax on other Masonic lodges – it would have been a vitally important shield, and doubtlessly considered very cheap at the price, particularly with a high-profile member of the royal family in the top slot. In addition, if the purpose was to ensure that Freemasonry wasn't seen as a seditious conspiracy, it is hardly any surprise that political and religious debate were so aggressively banned from lodge meetings, and that all specifics regarding religious belief were removed. If the movement had appeared partisan on the lethally dangerous Protestant–Catholic debate, it could have proved disastrous. Certainly, as the success of the Premier Grand Lodge of England became obvious, the rest of the British Isles was swift to join in. The Grand Lodge of Ireland was formed in 1725, and the Grand Lodge of Scotland wasn't far behind, in 1734. The first American Grand Lodge, the Grand Lodge of Pennsylvania, obtained its charter in 1731.

Meanwhile, the rituals and other details of the Craft were swiftly taking modern form. Many modern Masonic terms can be found in Scottish manuscripts from around the turn of the eighteenth century; other familiar terms found regular gleeful exposure in English press articles. The third degree of Master Mason was introduced some time around 1725, probably by a former Grand Master named John Theophilus Desaguliers. In 1730, the first book "exposing" Masonic rituals in detail was published: *Prichard's Masonry Dissected*. Until that point, the rituals had been passed on through rote learning, but Prichard's book actually served to stabilize the situation, and brought about greater uniformity. It is prized now among Masonic scholars as an insight into ritual development.

From the 1720s onward, Freemasonry spread swiftly across the world, carried by British soldiers, traders and expatriated settlers. A lot of Masonic work was also ongoing in France, where exiled and refugee Scots continued to meet in lodges. For quite some time, the French Masonic movement was used by Catholic Jacobite interests to plan further retaliations and revenge against the English state, but slowly the emphasis changed. There was certainly plenty of interest in retaining older ritual

Former Grand Master John Theophilus Desaguliers is generally thought to be the creator of the modern third-degree ceremony.

forms that had been used in the Scottish operative lodges, and this influence played a large part in the shaping of the Scottish Rite, which developed in France during the second quarter of the eighteenth century. The first three degrees of the Scottish Rite, which exist but are very rarely worked nowadays, are quite profoundly different in detail and structure to the traditional York Rite Blue degrees. Lodges and Grand Lodges, mostly warranted by one of the three British Grand Lodges or the Grand Orient d'France (1736), continued to sprout all over the world – stretching to China in 1767 and finally to Australia in 1820.

The Antients and Moderns

During this period, however, trouble was brewing among English Freemasons. The Premier Grand Lodge of England had established a major charitable wing in 1724. Thanks in part to the Industrial Revolution, it swiftly found itself pressed for alms by increasing waves of poor Masons from Ireland and Scotland. The situation was aggravated by Prichard's book, which had included the Masonic passwords, and a substantial number of fraudulent claims was also presented. The Grand Lodge reacted poorly to this tide, and unilaterally changed its

A typical Royal Arch breast jewel from 1924, gilded in silver, to be worn during gatherings of Royal Arch Masons.

ritual passwords and recognition signs. The new information was passed to all its regular lodges, but the Scots and Irish Masons, now covered by their own Grand Lodges (who did not receive the revised codes) found themselves unable to get into Masonic meetings or to apply for charitable aid.

The move – hardly following the Masonic spirit of charity – cost the Premier Grand Lodge of England a lot of goodwill, even from its own members. Over the next few years, a range of splinter groups sprang up, and English lodges that had not yet come under Grand Lodge's banner suddenly proved loathe to do so. Finally, in 1751, a group of lodges formed a rival body, calling themselves simply the Grand Lodge of England. They accused the Premier Grand Lodge of changing all manner of important details and losing the spirit of Freemasonry, and their charter reverted to the older forms that the migrant Masons could recognize – and benefit from. Because the new group felt they were using earlier, more established, material, they styled themselves as "The Antients", calling the older but updated group "The Moderns".

The Antients were quick to be generous to their previously disenfranchized brothers – and were quicker than the Moderns to admit members from the lower strata of society – and rapidly grew strong enough to be genuine rivals to the Premier Grand Lodge. Laurence Dermott, Grand Secretary of the Antients in 1756, proved highly influential, preparing constitutions and enlarging the recent Royal Arch ritual.

The Antients used the Royal Arch as a fourth degree, while the Moderns stuck to their three-degree status – but even that caused controversy. A fair number of Modern-affiliated Masons were sympathetic to the Royal Arch. Other degrees and revisions proliferated, not just between the bitterly divided Antients and Moderns, but with the Scottish Masons in France, the American lodges, and on and on. It has been estimated that at one point, there was as many as 1,400 different Masonic degrees being touted around, many with specific regional symbolism. The great majority were short-lived and utterly unimportant, but the situation did give a chance for the strongest influences in Masonry to be weeded out of the dross.

Indicating the rapid spread of Freemasonry, this 1730 board depicts charter sheets for all lodges under the Grand Lodge of England.

Finally, the two competing Grand Lodges were brought together. In 1813, the Earl of Moira spoke to the two rival Grand Masters, the Duke of Sussex (Moderns) and the Duke of Kent (Antients), and persuaded them to discuss the matter. This wasn't perhaps as impressive a feat as it might have been in other years – Sussex and Kent were brothers. A comparative group had been studying the differences between the two sides since 1809, so there was plenty of material to hand on what the differences actually were.

The two brothers sat down with a range of doctrinal experts, and decided a middle ground, often in favour of the Antients. The two Grand Lodges were then merged back together, forming the United Grand Lodge of England. A vast number of details and ritual elements had to be very quickly reconciled, but most of the regulations and ritual forms from that conclave still apply right across worldwide Freemasonry today – the schism between Anglo and Continental Freemasonry wasn't until 1868.

The Social Impact of Freemasonry

One of the very first things that all new Freemasons are taught is that it is vital to uphold the peace, avoid any action that might destabilize society and refrain from political discussion in the lodge. This is reinforced in the regulations that new Worshipful Masters have to swear, with the third injunction being never to get involved with a plot or conspiracy against the government. The Scottish Sinclair Charters directly acknowledge Crown patronage and the Buchanan Manuscript, dating from the mid-seventeenth century, charges Masons further to inform the king if they even hear of any treasonous activity. In the Anderson Constitutions, adopted by the Premier Grand Lodge of England, it specifically states that a Mason "is never to be concerned in plots and conspiracies against the peace and welfare of the Nation".

The prohibition is plain and absolute. But it doesn't sit very comfortably with historical record. The founding fathers of modern America – leaders of the revolution, drafters of the Constitution and the Bill of Rights, the first presidents – were proud rebels, and (for the most part) Freemasons. The principal political instigators in the early stages of French Revolution were Freemasons, and they even used its slogan of "Liberty, Equality, Fraternity". The wave of revolutions that swept Central and Latin America in the late eighteenth and nineteenth centuries was the work of Freemasons, including Simon Bolivar, Jose de San Martin, Vincente Guerrero and Benito Juarez. There is even a clause, deep in the constitutions, that says that a Freemason cannot be thrown out of the society for fomenting revolution, when any other illegal activity can be (and usually is) grounds for expulsion.

The simple truth is that Freemasonry, with its tenets of equality and fairness, has been a powerful agent of social change – even though its codes forbid any sort

The great rallying cry of the French Revolution was – like its ideals – taken whole from the teachings of Freemasonry.

of revolutionary role. As we have already discussed, the prohibitions on political change seem likely to have been put in place as protection against the Jacobite situation. Even so, this dual attitude requires some examination, as do the particular idea of liberty versus tyranny.

Politics and Power

If lodge records are anything to go by, liberty was a very important concern of eighteenth-century Freemasons. The word was particularly understood as the notion that the philosopher John Locke defined in his seminal *Two Treatises of Government*, written just before the end of the seventeenth century. Locke himself may or may not have been a Mason – the historical evidence is equivocal – but at the time it was certainly widely believed that he was. He was definitely a member of the Royal Society, which at the very least meant exposure to a lot of learned Freemasons and their ideas, and he was a good friend of Robert Boyle.

Locke suggested that good government is a trust, a contract to preserve the security of the citizen and his or her property. Political power has to balance with the essential liberty of the citizen. Without consent, Locke felt, there could be no obligation to civil obedience; when the trust failed, and law stopped enlarging freedom, but started restricting it, it was the citizen's right to decide that the trust had been breached. This was the cornerstone of his definition of liberty. Without it, the state was a tyranny – "the exercise of power beyond right". He argued that it was far better for a ruler to be opposed from time to time than for people to be tyrannized. When power is misused, Locke argued, the citizens are required to revolt.

Taking the Masonic proscriptions on face value, the implication is that a Freemason would have to respect and obey any political power, even the most vile tyrant or oppressor. This, however, is in direct contravention of the rest of Masonic teaching, which requires the freedom to grow and help others. Freemasonry is a doctrine that is geared around improvement of the self and of the world, and to lay down and accept tyranny goes against everything that it stands for. Only "free" people may become Freemasons, and in a dictatorship nobody is free. So, by its very definition, Freemasonry and tyranny are mutually exclusive. The only possible conclusion is that

In this painting, a group of Freemasons is shown sitting around socializing and debating the world's problems.

regardless of the exact letter of the constitutions, the proscriptions of obedience apply only to "legitimate" governments in Locke's sense – that is, those that uphold liberty. If the trust is broken, so is the proscription.

Regardless of the constitutions, however, a certain subversive streak was built into Freemasonry's very nature – from the point of view of the European monarchies of the time, anyway.

At the turn of the eighteenth century, Britain was in a unique position in Europe. Having had revolutions in 1640 and 1688, the country had moved from strict feudal royalism to the limited democracy of a parliamentary government. English Freemasonry kept very quiet during that period, to serve the demands of respectability. On the European continent, the Jacobite story of Freemasonry coming straight to France via Scotland was popular. That downplayed its English links – and the associated hints of revolutions, parliaments and democracies. Being English was automatically suspicious. Even playing up Scottish links, though, the Europeans suspected Freemasonry of having democratic intentions. When the Catholic Church condemned it in 1738, it was because it imitated certain aspects of republics – including the right to choose leaders and dismiss them later if necessary – which were deemed scandalous.

Debates and Doctrines

There is no denying that certain aspects of the new
British society were encoded into the Masonic
experience. Its members met sociably, as individuals,
divorced from the trappings and restrictions of their
status. Unlike all other social structures of the time –
family, school, church, venue and so on – Freemasonry
made no allowance for rank or social propriety. Social
life on the outside in Britain was considerably more
relaxed about interaction between social strata after
the seventeenth-century revolutions, but Freemasonry
was another level altogether.

For the most part, the Freemasons of the time were
drawn from the ranks of the educated, literate and at
least moderately wealthy top quarter to fifth of the male
population, who were also entitled to vote. Their chief
entertainments tended to be debating and lecturing,
often over heroic-sized meals and drinking sessions.
They were prepared to evaluate, discuss and hypothesize.
In the structures and constitutions of Freemasonry, they
created a fair form of government, complete with rights
and laws, and assigned it elections, representatives,
sovereignty and means of redress against it. In effect,
the lodges became functional training grounds in
successful democratic governments – and the men they
trained were precisely the sort to expound and theorize
to their friends.

By insisting on the doctrines of personal growth and
enlightenment, and by developing functional systems of
internal governance out of them, the lodges inadvertently
showed the most influential members of society how to
run a country fairly, with liberty. Bit by bit, the lodge
members became used to the ideas and dues of a free
citizen, rather than the lot of a bound subject – and they
saw them working, and working well, in every meeting.
Freemasonry never intended to be political – but then
politics, in that sense, specifically referred to partisan
political ideology, left wing versus right wing. Civic issues
were a different matter altogether. The struggle of liberty
versus tyranny was not considered political so much as
fundamental to the human need for freedom.

The idea of government by consent, within a
constitutional framework, establishing authority and
hierarchy without traditional privilege was implicit

In this highly allegorical and symbol-laden painting, the spirit
of Freemasonry is shown dispensing wisdom and information
to the people.

in the Masonic experience. Freemasonry didn't need to
allow political debate; by merely existing, it engaged in
political dialectic with its members. It was political, and
the culture it carried within it became known in Europe
as the Enlightenment.

Enlightenment thought held that the old ways were
irrational, choked with religious dogma and tradition
that supported privilege for its own sake. The way out
was through knowledge and fact, and study of the liberal
arts and sciences. Behind it all stood the doctrine of
reason. Logic had been around since the Greek
philosophers, but here it was combined with common
sense, direct observation, and a preference for freedom
and rational scepticism. Logic could easily be tied in
knots, or made to prove the absurd; while reason, faced
with absurdity, said so. Logic led to paradoxes such as
Xeno's tortoise, which should be arrow-proof because it

Above is a somewhat stylized depiction of a hooded candidate for initiation being led before the members of a French lodge.

would always have moved ahead slightly in the time the arrow took to catch up with it. Reason shook its head wearily and pointed out that when you shot something, the arrow hit, and that was that.

Global Expansion

By 1725, Freemasonry had established itself in France and Holland. The lodges embodied these strange new British cultural values, introducing the notions of tolerance, free socialization, the virtues of work and merit over birth, and government by constitution. The people who came to the lodges discovered that Enlightenment thought was inherent within them. There was no preaching or proselytizing, which would have almost certainly put newcomers off; just simple, practical demonstration of a system that worked. France was still feeling the effects of the death of Louis XIV in 1715 – the end of his 72-year reign was greeted with celebrations,

and the French nobility's fascination with the English fashions of the time made it easy for Freemasonry to become established.

French tastes were different to English ones, however. It was the deep historical mystery, allegory and noble spiritual aspirations of the Craft that appealed to the French peoples. The rites and mythic histories flourished there, and many new degrees were born. When Freemasonry became a firmly embedded part of social life in France, it was as a personal route to growth and exploration. To the English, Freemasonry was respectable; to the French, it was exciting. The influence of its thoughts and teachings could be seen all across French society. More than anything else though, Freemasonry brought a sense of social unity to the country.

France had long been a country of powerfully divided regions. Customs, superstitions and dialects changed regularly. Justice was local, class was a powerful divider, and even abstract notions, such as units of measurement and time, tended to differ. Freemasonry, however, was the same right across the country, offering welcome without prejudice regardless of class, religion, district or even nationality. The benefits of fellowship were obvious, and its spirit grew swiftly. Freemasonry and the Enlightenment quickly became a dominant social force, giving people an alternative to the repressive stagnancy of the old ways.

French Freemasonry never had a conscious goal of revolution. As in England, though, its structures and mores demonstrated better ways, and the French people listened to it. The basic Masonic principles of equality, fraternity and liberty became touchstones of a population whose rulers were famously out of touch with reality. The idea of accepting equality in front of a greater system, a fair system, led to a sea change in the intellectual and social structure of the country. The aristocracy had shown that it could be a harmonious part of a working whole on an equal footing to everyone else.

Ultimately, when the French revolution came it swept most of the nobility away – the years of resentment were too powerful to contain. Buoyed by the French example, the age of reason spread across Europe, shaping the world as it is today. One of the greater ironies is that in Britain, careless revolutionary fervour had led to a

halfway house of federalization. The nation remained
a Kingdom and kept its nobility, even though the royal
power was greatly curtailed by the will of the people.
The mild nature of English revolution helped create
Freemasonry, but the ideas, exported to the Continent,
gained a weight and urgency that they did not have back
in London. While the great majority of the European
monarchies were swept away by the Enlightenment,
Britain's remains intact and constitutionally functional.

Meanwhile, in the USA, the situation among the
thirteen colonies was even more divisive than it had
been in France. The colonies had entirely separate
governments, different religious tendencies, widely
separate social standards, and highly disparate national
origins. All of them were fiercely independent, and all
jealous of each other. Once again, Freemasonry was the
sole point of common contact. It spread rapidly among
the higher social strata, for the same reasons that it had
done elsewhere – it offered a point of contact, some
structure, and a social outlet – and it carried the same
lessons. Brotherhood. Equality. Fairness. As members of

**Master Freemason Benjamin Franklin is shown here with
colleagues, drafting the American Declaration of Independence.**

the colonies travelled from region to region – merchants,
soldiers, other officials – they found that the lodges
provided a place of guaranteed welcome and fellow
feeling. The most philanthropic members of the society
would typically be found to have already gravitated to a
lodge, and advice, local information and even assistance
were always forthcoming. Slowly, the lodges introduced
something totally new between the colonies: a feeling of
American unity.

The first great advocate of Freemasonry in the
colonies was Benjamin Franklin. In organizing his
colony-wide news, he gained a strong mouthpiece for
promoting Masonic ideals. From 1750 on, the British
government tried harder and harder to encroach on the
colonies, which served to help unite them against it. The
idea of national unity gained strength, and Freemasonry
was in the vanguard as the only real outlet for exchanging
views between the colonies.

As is well known now, Boston was the flashpoint. The
puritan merchants there already resented the English,
and were incensed by the taxes and restrictions on their
trade. St Andrew's lodge of Boston met in a tavern called
the Green Dragon Inn, and in 1773 its Worshipful Master
was a surgeon named Joseph Warren, a close personal
friend of Benjamin Franklin. Fellow lodge members
included Paul Revere and John Hancock. On the
afternoon of December 16, a bunch of masked men burst
out of the Green Dragon and marched to the harbour,
where they boarded a group of English merchant ships
and tossed almost 350 cases of English tea overboard.
They then returned to the Green Dragon, singing
cheerfully. Their identities were never discovered, but the
minutes of St Andrew's Lodge show that there was a
meeting at the tavern that afternoon – and nothing more.

As the American Revolution kicked off, it was largely
the will and spirit of George Washington that held the
colonial army together. Undersupplied, untrained,
hungry and barefoot, it was Washington who drove the
revolution. A long-standing Mason, he was known to
refer to Freemasonry's cross-colony influence as "the
cement which binds us together". There were military
lodges across the colonial army as well, and Washington
is said to have visited them all personally, helping them
to inspire courage, hope and morale.

The Boston Tea Party that sparked the American War of Independence: Could this famous revolutionary action have been undertaken by Masons from the Green Dragon Inn?

In the meantime, Benjamin Franklin went to France to seek practical assistance in the conflict. Faced with sympathetic apathy from the French, Franklin joined a new, influential lodge known as The Lodge of the Nine Sisters, and then persuaded the group to initiate Voltaire, the hero of the French public. At the end of the ceremony, the two men embraced, and the story became so retold that soon the two men were being asked to demonstrate their embrace each time they appeared together in public. Franklin manipulated the publicity and ongoing interest masterfully, and finally won the public over. The aid that the colonies needed was swiftly forthcoming.

After the war had finished, the men who shaped the Constitution and the Bill of Rights were mostly Freemasons. They did their best to enshrine Masonic principles of genuine fairness and liberty into an unassailable charter. That it took nearly two hundred years for business and government to wear those principles away is an amazing testament to the influence that Freemasonry had on American society.

Everywhere in the world that it settled, Freemasonry introduced the concepts of equality, brotherhood and liberty. Those ideas, too powerful to contain, inevitably spilled out as reform, revolution, social change. They inspired Simon Bolivar to liberate six whole countries from the rule of the Spanish. Despite its strict prohibition on political debate, Freemasonry's very nature has given it a central role worldwide in spreading social reform and liberty.

3

Symbolism, Freemasonry's Sacred Heart

The journey into Freemasonry's symbolic teachings is one that can last a lifetime. The depth and richness of the core degrees alone would take book upon book to explore properly. When you add in the influences of the different historical and mystical traditions that underpin the Craft, the complexities become so subtle that precise objective interpretation becomes impossible. Freemasonry is of necessity a personal journey for each member. However, the symbolism and teachings of the three degrees – both literal and symbolic – represent the structure and journey of Masonry's sacred mysteries. All that the candidate needs to know is captured within them. Together, they form a coherent, majestic whole: the same lesson that has been taught in mystery schools throughout the world and across history.

The central decoration of this Scottish Rite apron symbolizes the entire heart of Freemasonry and the mysteries and wonders it contains.

The Entered Apprentice

Traditionally, nobody should be invited in to Freemasonry; the prospective member is supposed to have enough interest in the society to ask for membership. Originally, you had to ask three times on separate occasions, and the Mason you asked was not supposed even to acknowledge the question the first two times – a serious test of powerful interest. That has fallen by the wayside, but still it is common for members to hint about membership to friends and colleagues rather than to broach the subject outright. This is symbolically represented by the notion that a new member is first made a Mason inside his own heart.

Before first entry to the lodge, the candidate is "prepared" by setting aside a range of different things, and by putting on a number of symbolic garments and other items. This preparation is an act of faith and good intent, and symbolically reduces the candidate to just his own self, free of status, wealth or social trapping. He is expected to enter the lodge free of disturbing influences – from certain metals through to his prejudices and uncontrolled passions. When fully prepared, there remains the last act of seeking admission – taking the active rather than passive role.

The Great Lights of Masonry

Stepping into the lodge is a serious action, of course. Moving into the "Light of Freemasonry" brings with it genuine consequences. The new candidate becomes an apprentice, and there is work to be done, as there is in any craft. Advances and rewards are earned, and members are given tools, not toys. The candidate's joyous welcome in the lodge symbolizes the seriousness of that step. It must be taken thoughtfully, not rashly; with bravery, not cowardice.

During the period of the initiation ceremony, the candidate is walked around the lodge several times in a series of set patterns and circumambulations. This serves several purposes. On a literal level, it allows the lodge members to examine the candidate and make sure that he is prepared. Symbolically, it represents the path of the sun through the sky, along with the idea of walking through a labyrinth that separates the worthy from the unworthy, and also acts to align the candidate properly with the inner world of the lodge.

Eventually, the candidate comes to the altar. At the heart of the lodge as God is at the heart of Masonry, the altar symbolizes faith, light, God's blessing, worship and obligation. The oath that the candidate takes at the altar is, therefore, seen as being taken in front of God as well as the lodge, and is thus doubly binding. The oath itself conveys the duties, rights and expectations of the candidate; at a deeper level, it also represents a personal relationship with God – in earlier times, such compacts with one's deity were common.

On the altar, the candidate comes face to face with the Great Lights of Masonry for the first time – the Volume of Sacred Law, the Square and the Compass. In the English-speaking world, it is usually the case that the King James Bible will be used as the Volume of Sacred Law. A candidate is expected to inform the lodge if his personal belief requires a different scriptural book, which will then be provided. Lodges whose members are predominantly non-Christian will naturally use other books. Symbolically, the open Bible is a reminder to let our faith guide our conduct and our interactions with others, and also serves to highlight the importance of man's relation to the divine. The Square symbolizes honesty, truth and morality, and has become a linguistic symbol worldwide for fairness – "square dealing", "on the level", "all square", "fair and square" and so on. The Compass, by comparison, symbolizes skill, knowledge and restraint. It is also a token of exclusion – harmful and selfish things are banished beyond the barrier of the circle, ensuring good faith inside.

The conjoined Square and Compass – depicted in some territories with a "G" in the centre, for "God" and/or "Geometry" (or just possibly "Gematria") – is the most famous of all Masonic symbols. Brought together on the Book, with the Square representing stone and earth and the Compass representing the arcs of heaven, the combined triple symbol is a reminder of God's will in the creation of heaven and earth. The three-part nature of the symbol can also be seen as paralleling the three symbolic degrees, referring the first, second and third degrees to the body, mind and soul (for the Square, Compass and Book), respectively – and also back to the three conscious worlds of the Kabbalah.

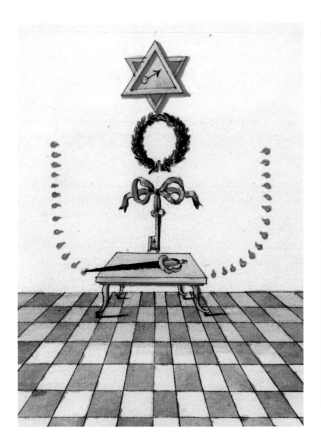

This artistic depiction of a Masonic altar draws on some of the deepest symbolism of the Craft.

Blazoned on a book, the square and compass together symbolize God's will and mastery in the creation of the Earth and heavens.

The Apron and the Tools

Following the Great Lights, the candidate is presented with the second most famous symbol in Freemasonry – the Masonic apron. Initially presented as a plain white lambskin envelope, the apron symbolizes innocence, virtue, rebirth, work and the builder's craft, as well as linking back to the concept of initiation in a whole swathe of historical Greek and Egyptian mystery cults. It also has a range of other associations, through more arcane links, to purification, sacrifice, energy and growth. With its simple shape of a rectangle surmounted by a triangle, it also embodies the symbolism of the numbers 4 and 3, and together 7 – numbers that link recurrently to all the critical Masonic themes.

After being given his apron, the new apprentice is shown the set of working tools by which, supposedly, the early professional stoneworkers of his grade would have worked. More importantly, their symbolic power lies in indicating how and where the apprentice can begin to improve himself. Each degree has its own working tools, and their nature reflects the nature of the self-improvement work flagged up in that degree.

The tools of the apprentice are the 24-inch gauge and the common gavel. The gauge is a ruler, broken into three folding sections representing the day, and the way that our time should be used – eight hours for our regular work, eight hours for worship, charity, self-perfection and aiding the distressed, and eight hours for sleep. The common gavel is a stone hammer used to chip off rough edges. The symbolism here could hardly be plainer. The work of the apprentice is to chip off his own rough edges, eliminating vices and gratuitous

A highly decorated Worshipful Master on his throne. His gavel is a symbol of his authority over the lodge, and the globes on the top of his chair supports transform them into symbols of the Pillars of Solomon.

indulgences. Note that taken together, one tool is passive, calculating and measuring, for deciding what needs to be kept, while the other is active, applying force, getting rid of the rest.

The Immovable and Movable Jewels

After the tools are presented, the apprentice is symbolically placed in the northeast corner of the lodge. This is because, traditionally, the northeast corner is where a building's cornerstone (the first stone laid) is placed. The apprentice becomes his own living cornerstone, the foundation on which he will found the temple of his soul. Masonry considers the north to be the place of darkness, and the east the source of light, so by placing the apprentice in that corner, the lodge is also confirming that he is approaching the light, but has not yet fully attained it.

In this point, the symbolism of the lodge is explained by the Worshipful Master, from certain details of the meeting room through to the cardinal virtues of Freemasonry. In shape, the lodge room is (ideally) an oblong in the form of two cubes placed next to each other, with its length running east to west, and its width north to south. Above, its roof depicts the canopies of heaven. The Master sits in the east, as he is the source of wisdom and instruction.

The supports of the lodge – the three pillars of wisdom, strength and beauty – are shown to correspond to the three Lesser Lights of the primary officers (Worshipful Master, Senior Warden and Junior Warden, respectively) and also to the so-called immovable jewels. These are the square (morality), level (equality) and plumb line (goodness) – each virtue springing from the traits of the pillars. They also represent the three ancient Grand Masters: King Solomon as the eidolon of wisdom; King Hiram of Tyre as the strength that enabled the building of the temple; and Hiram Abiff because his skill beautified the temple and its adornments.

The afternoon sun blazes through the west-facing windows of this beautiful, classically designed lodge room. This is the view the Worshipful Master would enjoy from his seat in the east.

In addition to the immovable jewels, there are also three movable jewels: the rough ashlar, the perfect ashlar and the trestleboard. "Ashlar" is a term for a building stone; the trestleboard originally held the architect's plans. They represent the process of initiation through the three degrees of Masonry – from the rough, unprepared form of the apprentice to the cleaned and perfected virtue of the fellowcraft, and thus to the Master Mason's work of building the temple in his own soul.

The lodge's ornaments – as revealed on the first-degree tracing board, which is a large, symbol-rich image on board or carpet – are said to be the mosaic pavement, the indented tassel and the blazing star. The pavement – a chequerboard of black and white – is symbolic of the world, with its good and evil, ease and pain, love and hate, progress and restriction. It is the vale of tears that we must make our way through. The indented tassel surrounding it represents the blessings and comforts that make the world bearable and that we hope to earn, with the aid of the blazing star – divine provenance.

Instruction of the First Degree

Finally, the apprentice is told of the three tenets of Freemasonry, its four cardinal virtues, and the three prima materia of the entered apprentice. The tenets and virtues aren't really symbolic issues as such, so much as direct moral instruction. The tenets are brotherly love (see all humanity as one family), relief (sincere compassion and a ready ear for the unhappy) and truth (be good and sincere). The cardinal virtues are temperance, fortitude, prudence and justice.

Lastly, the materia, with which apprentices are said to have served their masters, are chalk, charcoal and clay. These are said to represent freedom, fervency and zeal,

Divine provenance is represented by the five-pointed blazing star. At its centre, the eye of God looks out over all, alluding to the bounty and power of God's love.

The lodge ornaments – tassel, blazing star and chequerboard – form a critical framework for this symbolic illustration of Masonic principle.

respectively. Chalk is free because it leaves traces on almost any surface with just the lightest touch; charcoal is fervent because it is capable, when ignited, of overcoming and melting even the stubbornest metals; and clay is zealous because it supports us continually without falter (as earth in general), brings forth that which we need, and serves as a constant reminder of our mortality.

Overall, the first degree is about the critical work of self-mastery. It symbolizes the transition from childhood to adulthood, when we truly learn that although we will always be the heroes of our own stories, the world itself doesn't revolve around us; indeed, it won't even notice our passing. The work required in this degree is that of control and purification; the tools given are those needed to bring the body and its whims and urges under the control of the Mason. We must learn to master our drives, to

Illuminated above the Mason's head, the equilateral triangle – all sides and angles the same – symbolizes the strength and unity of the parts that make the whole complete.

make them work for us rather than to be made to work for them. Only then will we have the necessary patience and steadiness to take the next step.

The Fellowcraft

If the first degree is centred around mastering the emotions and baser impulses, the teachings of the second degree are all about gathering knowledge. As well as a worthy end in and of itself, the idea is also that greater knowledge will provide new tools by which the Mason can improve his character and the society in which he lives. In particular, the Fellowcraft is directed toward the classical liberal arts and sciences, historically considered those that would lead to the development of the mind. The Fellowcraft degree is about more than just the benefits of a broad education, though – it is about perfecting the mind and bringing it under the control of the personality, just as the first degree is about perfecting drives and emotions and bringing them under control. Only a person in mastery of himself can hope to begin the final work of perfecting the spirit. In general, where the symbolism of the first degree suggests rebirth, first steps and youth, the second degree as a whole symbolizes the transition into spiritual adulthood, with symbols of passage, advancement and elevation.

Once again, the candidate for elevation is "duly and truly" prepared outside the lodge. The manner of preparation bears similarities to the first degree, but with notable differences. All through the degree structure, one of the most dominant recurrent themes is the number three. It is worth noting at this point that symbolically and geometrically, three represents the triangle. Furthermore, there are three types of triangle by side, and three types of triangle by angle. By side, the equilateral triangle has all sides the same, the isosceles triangle has two sides the same, and the scalene has no sides the same. By angle, an obtuse triangle has its largest angle greater than 90 degrees, a right-angled triangle has its largest angle exactly 90 degrees, and an acute triangle has its largest angle less than 90 degrees. The different interrelations of the triangles and the patterns in which three things can occur overlap quite notably with certain elements of the preparation, as well as with other groups and combinations of three in the lodge detail.

The Square, the Level and the Plumb Line

The working tools assigned to the Fellowcraft are the three immovable jewels of the lodge. The square is the perfect measure of critical accuracy – its two sides meet at exactly 90 degrees, known as a right angle. This name doesn't come from turning toward the right-hand side; rather, it comes from the fact that it is the only stable angle at which a line (therefore a wall) can stand under its own weight. Even the slightest variance means that the weight of a free (lone) wall is not centred, and sooner or later it will collapse. This accuracy is symbolically extended out to rectitude, honesty, truthfulness and morality in general.

The second tool, the level, symbolizes equity. Regardless of accidents of birth (status, talent, strengths and weaknesses and so on), every person is a child of the divine and can aspire to any height. All are equal, and such trifles as wealth and social status are irrelevant – just distractions from the work of the soul. Thus, the level reminds us that work – particularly the great work of purification and improvement – is the source of dignity.

The plumb line is traditionally used to check that a structure is built straight and true. By direct analogy, it is a symbol of upright behaviour, of righteousness. God told the prophet Amos that he would set a plumb line in the middle of his people; in Freemasonry, this is considered a symbolic warning to judge a person by their own standards of right and wrong, rather than by your own – in other words, to discard any personal prejudices. As a personal measure, the plumb line becomes a metaphor for the conscience and the most basic sense of justice – that of treating each person fairly.

Forever upright, measuring accuracy and verity, the plumb line is a reminder for the most elemental conscience and justice.

The Temple Pillars

Certain elements of the mythic design of King Solomon's temple are important symbolic tools in this degree. In the previous degree, it is assumed that the lodge is de facto operating in one of the ground-floor alcoves set in the temple walls. For the second degree, the lodge is, instead, thought to be in the middle chamber, which means ascending a winding staircase up to the second level.

At the entrance to King Solomon's temple, two bronze pillars were placed, symbolizing strength and establishment. These are represented symbolically in all Masonic lodges, and imply power channelled into effective action. Without control, power is destructive anarchy; without power, control is irrelevant. The two must be twinned if life is to proceed. It has been suggested that, historically, the two pillars might have originally represented the twin pillars – the Pillar of Cloud and the Pillar of Fire – that guided the Israelites to the promised land. Other historians have suggested that they formed a gateway between profane and sacred space, or any number of other possible dualities. In light of their Masonic interpretation, the twin pillars offer a rich vein of material for

Jacob's three steps to heaven, corresponding to faith, hope and charity, are represented still in the first stage of the middle chamber stair.

contemplation. They are topped with globes, which in Masonic thought are said to represent the spheres of earth and heaven.

The Staircase

The winding staircase, which gave access to the upper levels of alcoves in the temple outer walls, sat at the corner of Solomon's temple. In Masonry, it is a complex, multi-layered symbol of ascension. Nowadays, it is typically divided into three stages: the first of three steps, the second of five steps, and the third of seven steps.

The first three steps are representative of the three degrees and, by extension, the body-mind-soul grouping, the three principal officers of the lodge, the three traditional theological virtues of faith, hope and charity, and so on. Originally, these were the steps, or vertical methods of ascension, on Jacob's Ladder that led to heaven. It is interesting to note the complimentary nature of the four cardinal virtues of the first degree, which are intrinsically linked to the four horizontal directions of the compass – guides to action on earth, as the theological virtues are guides to rising to heaven. The four-and-three symbolism also links back to the square and triangle of the Masonic apron. All is linked.

The second set of steps, the five, are said to be the five orders of classical architecture. The architectural orders were systems by which proportions, ornamentations and member parts of a column were arranged and, by extension, systems for the regular arrangement of an entire building in order to form a coherent whole. The original orders were the three Greek orders, Doric, Ionic and Corinthian. Each was whole, different and possessed unique characteristics. The Romans added two more orders, which were basically minor alterations to the Greek modes. The Composite was like Corinthian but with added ornamentation in the Ionic mode, while the Tuscan, similar to Doric but with less ornamentation, was supposed, therefore, to be earlier.

The three Greek orders are particularly valued, because they have originality that the Roman orders lack. In addition to this primary reference, the steps also refer to the human senses: sight, sound, touch, taste and smell. As with the architectural correspondence, there are three senses that are particularly prized, and two that are less important – sight, sound and touch are deemed essential, for they allow a member to perceive the signs, words and grips of recognition, while smell and taste are considered less critical. Certainly in life itself, lacking sight, sound or touch is a major disability, while to be without smell or taste is a personal tragedy, but no bar to almost full functioning. Therefore, the five steps carry with them an implication of three-and-two. This links back to the symbol of the pentacle as the microcosm of man, to the uneven duality of sun over moon, and so on. Once again, there a deep veins of symbolism contained in this issue.

The third grouping, the seven steps, are a depiction of the seven classical liberal arts and sciences. These are traditionally listed as grammar, rhetoric, logic, arithmetic, geometry, music and astronomy. Geometry, as previously noted, is particularly prized among Masons. Figuratively, it is critical for an architect who needs to plan and execute designs, or for an engineer to prepare land for working. Without geometry, architecture is impossible, and astronomy and arithmetic are considerably weakened. The liberal arts and sciences date back to as early as the fourth century AD, and were at their height in the twelfth century, at which point they were considered a route to the greater understanding of God – their depictions can be found sculpted on the west door of the Cathedral of Chartres in France. It was in Chartres that it was decided, for the first time, that a stonemason who had mastered the seven arts was entitled to call himself an architect.

In this seal, the greater is mirrored in the lesser, the macrocosm in the microcosm; and so the study of science is a route to understanding God.

Over the course of the winding staircase, the candidate makes the passage from the outer porch to the middle chamber. In terms of Masonic legend, having the right to climb the stairs was a mark of distinction, with increased wages. As the intellectual and spiritual lessons gel and the member develops, he is said to be gradually opening the doors to the middle chamber internally, in his own mind.

The Three Wages and the Three Jewels

Inside the middle chamber, the Fellowcraft receives symbolic wages due his station – corn, wine and oil, a reflection of the tithe paid by Solomon to Hiram of Tyre in return for his materials and experts. This suggests, notionally, that the candidate is aligned with the Tyrians rather than with the locals. The three wages together symbolize mental and spiritual plenty, and the many powerful intangible rewards of living a good life.

Overtly, corn (wheat) is nourishment – the staff of life – but on a slightly deeper level it also symbolizes plenty, giving and service. Traditionally, wheat is also used to fashion representations of the cornucopia, or horn of plenty. Goodness-laden horns of that sort were thought to bring crop fertility and rich harvests. Wine symbolizes refreshment and health, ease, peace, and by allusion to the transubstantiation, spirituality and blessing. Oil is said to stand for joy, happiness and glad times.

Finally, the new Fellowcraft is also instructed regarding the three jewels of the degree – the attentive ear, the instructive tongue, and the faithful breast. These are fairly shallow symbolically, and refer simply to the process and techniques of learning. Only by increasing knowledge and gaining the breadth and perspective to exalt the mind can the Fellowcraft attain mastery.

Although these jewels are unsubtle, they are very indicative. The second degree is about the journey of adulthood. The purpose of this period is to learn, and in doing so expand the mind to the point where it is able to start enlightening. The liberal arts and sciences were originally chosen specifically for their ability to expand the intellect and its capacity for spiritual understanding. All through the ceremony, the imagery is very tightly focused on learning and intellectual work. This is the foundation degree, and preparation must be completed on the work of dedicating the mind and body as the temple of the soul.

Give us this day our daily bread – corn symbolizes not only day-to-day nourishment, but also the associated virtues of generosity and helpfulness. Sheafs of corn (wheat) are shown on this Mason's apron surrounding the symbolic centre.

The Master Mason

The third degree is the moment at which all the candidate's work in self-mastery and enlightenment is realized. Symbolically – if not actually – the candidate has brought his inner natures into balance with each other and with his higher, spiritual self. He is physically purified, mentally sharpened and intellectually broadened. In this state, he is ready to approach the sublime degree, that of Master Mason. In practice, of course, it is very rare for any individual actually to take the time (and effort) required to reach such an advanced state before seeking ascendancy to the third. Effectively, the ceremony of the third degree becomes an outer representation of the inner rewards waiting for a Mason who completes the work of the first and second degrees. The journey of mastery is an ongoing one, however much we might wish otherwise.

At the start of the ceremony, the candidate enters in darkness, as before. There is a difference though, in that his preparations have left him in a state of balanced

The hawk-headed Egyptian deity Horus, son of Osiris, is shown here holding an Ankh, the symbol of rebirth.

equilibrium, with greater confidence and complete faith in the Great Lights. After the initial ceremonies, which are reminiscent of earlier rituals, the candidate takes the centre role in a dramatic re-enactment of the central legend of Freemasonry.

The Act of Death and Rebirth

Over the course of this section, the candidate plays the part of Hiram Abiff, chief architect of Solomon's temple. In a dramatic ceremony, the candidate is figuratively slain as Abiff was murdered. Afterwards, the candidate is raised back into himself from his symbolic role as Abiff, leaving his impurities and flaws behind. This cycle of figurative death and rebirth is found in all of the historical mystery schools; it is the cleansing that allows us to transcend our prior flaws. This symbolism is ancient and easily traced back thousands of years. The candidate is reborn into a new spiritual consecration, cleansed and purified to open the way to mastery.

There are close parallels between the Hiramic legend and the legends of the Egyptian god Osiris, the Greek god Dionysius and even, tangentially, some of the Norse legends of Odin. In each case, the dominant theme is sacrifice and rebirth. Hiram, of course, is not reborn in the legend, but the Master Mason's rising out of the role and back into himself makes a close parallel. In the sense of Hiram's soul rising to Heaven and leaving his impure clay behind, so there is also the raising of the new Master back into the light of God's love, leaving his impure and gross nature behind. As an interesting aside, there is of course no Masonic suggestion of any divinity on the part of Hiram Abiff, but while he is refusing to reveal his secrets to his murderers, he explains that he could not do so without his two fellow-masters – King Solomon and King Hiram of Tyre. This could be a subtle reference to the Holy Trinity and to other historic tripartite depictions of divinity – an allusion that it is not possible to understand the divine truth if it is fragmented.

The ruffians themselves primarily symbolize the simple truth that trying to attain spiritual wisdom by any method other than earning it is simultaneously futile, stupid and destructive. The reward can only be earned, it cannot be stolen or extorted. As idioms for our own ignorance, laziness and greed, they represent base

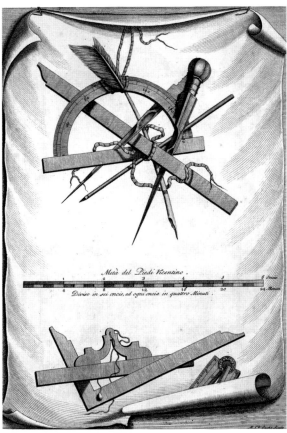

The awesome destructive power of lightning was harnessed into Thor's hammer, represented as the maul that killed Hiram Abiff.

The pencil, skirret (pin and straight market) and compass are tools by which a Master Mason should seek to perfect himself.

passions that can quite literally destroy us if we do not take pains to keep them subdued and under control. There is no truth or life eternal in greed, just death.

The maul, the finally effective weapon used by the third ruffian, is a large wooden hammer used to bed finished stone firmly into a wall. It has also been symbolic of destruction since the very earliest times. Thor's hammer is a mighty weapon capable of levelling mountains if required; it contains all the power of the thunder and lightning associated with him. As a weapon with which to attack Hiram Abiff, it represents that sheer destructive power.

The Lion of Judah was the sign of the royal tribe of the Hebrew nation. Each king, in turn, became the new Lion of Judah both literally and figuratively. It would have been one of Solomon's titles. As a symbol, the lion stands for

royalty, power, grace, the sun and sheer might. In medieval times, it was also a sign of resurrection – a widely known tale described a stillborn cub that lay dead three days before its father breathed on it, and it returned to life.

Acacia is a powerful Middle Eastern symbol of immortality and endurance, and is planted at the head of graves to represent this. As a durable evergreen, it links survival, indomitability and sometimes even rebirth with simpler notions of innocence. It is a common belief that the crown of thorns was made of acacia.

In due course, the candidate is raised to the "sublime degree" of Master Mason. This raising is quite literal; the candidate is lifted away from his role as Abiff and back to himself. His time embodying the Master brings Mastery – his imperfections are left behind.

The Tools and Symbols

As the new Master Mason is invested, he is given the working tools of the degree by which he may turn his new spiritual focus toward the purification of his soul. The tools are the skirret, pencil and compass. A skirret is basically a pin at the centre of a straight marker. The pin can be stuck into the ground to provide a well-oriented line, and symbolically reminds the Master of the straight line of good conduct as laid down by religious teaching and proscription. The pencil would have been used in planning and drawing instructions for the builders, but it also stands for the notable fact that all our actions are observed, and we will have to account for them after our lives. The compass, finally, is required to calculate limits, proportions and arcs, and to permit accuracy and precision, which, symbolically, stand for the unerring and impartial justice of divine judgement.

Alternatively, in some areas the Master Mason is said to have as working tools all the equipment of Freemasonry. However, in these cases the degree is specifically said to be associated with the trowel, symbolizing the cementing of ties and the spreading of brotherly love.

Finally, a last set of symbols associated with the specific icons on the Master's carpet are explained to the new Master Mason. The figure of the three steps

Beehives are an important Masonic symbol referring to industry, dedication, productivity, good works and the power of all pulling together.

represents both the stages of human life and the degrees of the Craft; the parallels between the two are both overt and intentional. As children and Entered Apprentices, we are ruled by our whims and instincts, and it is our task to prepare ourselves for adulthood by learning control. As adults and Fellowcrafts, we have enough control to begin acquiring the knowledge that can enrich us personally, and to the successful discharge of our duties to God. Finally, with old age and mastery comes wisdom and the happy knowledge of the immortality of the soul.

The incense pot represents purity of heart, which is inherently a suitable sacrifice to the divine. Symbolically, it reminds us to be grateful to the divine for our existence and blessings. The beehive is a famous and international image of hard work and industriousness, and so reminds us of the importance of application. By extension, it also warns us not to sit idle and self-satisfied when there are those around us who are in need, particularly if our aid will cost us little.

The Book of Constitutions watched over by the Tyler's sword is a reminder to be cautious and guarded in our words and actions. The heart watched over by the pointing sword is a reminder of divine justice – justice that sees all and remembers all. It is an encouragement to remain virtuous, for the reward is sure. The ark and anchor represent a life well lived, and hope well founded. The symbolic link back to Noah is obvious; virtue brings safety, and anchors the soul in righteousness in preparation for its final reward.

Euclid's forty-seventh problem is better known as Pythagoras's theorem – in any right-angled triangle, the ratios of the triangle's sides will be in the proportion 3:4:5, with the longest side being opposite the right-angle. More mathematically, the formula described states that for a scalar triangle, the square of the hypotenuse is equal to the sum of the squares of the other two sides. This particular mathematical curiosity just so happens to be one of the most practically vital discoveries in architecture and geometry. With this knowledge and thin rods 3, 4 and 5 units in length, you can construct a perfect right-angle every time. Like some of the other geometric wonders – *pi*, the golden ratio and the Fibonacci

series – it is of quite literally world-changing importance. Its presence is a reminder of the importance of the liberal arts and sciences, as well as a symbolic statement that some things that seem crippled are, in fact, the most vital perfection there is.

Life, Death and Immortality

The hourglass and the scythe represent the short duration of human life and the importance of time. The maul, discussed earlier, is found again here; it also represents accidents and diseases, which can cut life short. The spade is an emblem of digging, particularly graves. The coffin, finally, is the last resting place of our earthly shell. To stop all these plain symbols getting overpoweringly morbid, these tokens of mortality are finished off with a sprig of acacia, reminding us that mortality is a matter of the body only, and that the immortal soul will continue on – but that is a matter for the individual and his own relationship with his faith and his version of divinity.

The third degree is the ceremony of initiation, the passage from mundane consciousness into enlightenment. Without perfect preparation in the first two degrees, the experience will remain "just going through the motions" – but then again, when you are ready, enlightenment will come. It is the secret at the heart of all mystery schools, the journey of all esoteric traditions. Over the course of the ceremony, the candidate embodies an enlightened master. The death that follows is partly to symbolize the passing of old concerns, and partly to symbolize the crossing into enlightenment – the state of being awake to the oh-so-subtle needs and urgings of the soul. We come back to ourselves, carrying something of the enlightened master back with us to a greater or lesser extent. Once the state of mastery is attained, the great work itself can begin – working with the soul to build a pure temple to God inside ourselves. This is the work of the Master Mason, the point that all the symbolism leads to, and there is no more exalted task.

Maiden, Mother and Crone – the three ages of mankind correspond closely to the three degrees of Freemasonry. The hourglass and scythe are reminders of human mortality.

4

Freemasonry Today

Freemasonry has come a long way in the last three hundred years, and not all of it is good. Since hitting its peak strength after the Second World War, the Craft has been in notable decline. It isn't alone in that, of course – these are highly pressured, secular times and most of the older institutions are shrinking rapidly. The fact remains, however, that Freemasonry faces a critical challenge in the years ahead if it is to survive in any meaningful sense. Its demise would be a tragic shame, since the world needs to heed its lessons of unity and decency now more than ever.

The Volume of the Sacred Law comes before all others as UGLE's Grand Lodge officers file past in 1992.

Ugly Sisters

One of the greatest blows that the twentieth century dealt Freemasonry was the gradual erosion of its reputation. In the eighteenth and nineteenth centuries, Masonry had been viewed as an honourable, even noble pursuit, a thing of pride and social status to be involved in. Its role in bringing liberty and enlightenment was well known and the Craft was considered a highly beneficial organization. That changed over the twentieth century, as a new attitude of paranoia and hostility crept into society at large.

Freemasonry, as an organization that sought to keep some secrets, was immediately suspect. Small-minded reporters and other critics, incapable of imagining that people might actually seek to better themselves, decided that it had to be a cover for corrupt business dealings and nepotism. Some religious zealots declared that the secrecy hid satanic rituals and a conspiracy of international evil. The women's movement, very aware of any institution that remained male-only, was quick to condemn the whole thing as terminally sexist and out of touch, a dull old-boys' club for latent homosexuals and misogynists. A couple of financial scandals featuring former Masons helped add a brimstone whiff of conspiracy.

Throughout it all, Freemasonry as a whole remained aloof toward the charges, unimpressed and refusing to dignify them with an answer. Unfortunately, this was probably a mistake; in the eyes of the public, silence was tantamount to confession. The hysteria peaked in the late 1980s, and in some areas only enshrined constitutional rights kept Freemasonry from being devastated by hostile governmental policies. The furore has died down now, but Masonry has been badly tarnished.

Propaganda Due

The most damaging of all the Masonic-related scandals was undoubtedly the Roberto Calvi affair. Propaganda Due (or P2), constituted under the Grand Orient of Italy, is probably the most infamous Masonic lodge in modern history – despite the fact that it was closed before ever becoming notorious, and its Machiavellian Grand Master, Licio Gelli, expelled. The irony is clear for all to see; Freemasonry's most damaging scandal is the responsibility of a man who had already been thrown out of the Craft for gross misconduct.

Licio Gelli was born in 1919. He volunteered for Mussolini's fascist expeditionary force at the age of 17, and was sent to Spain. From there, he became a liaison officer to the armies of the Third Reich. At the end of the Second World War, he quickly took his military and criminal contacts to the CIA, helping to smuggle Klaus Barbi over to the USA. He then became part of the CIA's anti-communist "fifth column" of traitors, Operation Gladio, who would remain across Europe to work against Russia in the event of an invasion. With access to information – dirty secrets, confidential business plans and so on – that the relationship gave him, he was swiftly able to become rich and influential.

The gorgeous classical buildings of the Vatican dominate Rome's beautiful skyline.

Roberto Calvi (centre) faces a court in Milan in 1981, just months before his murder in London.

The P2 lodge was consecrated in 1895, but, like many Italian organizations, it was infiltrated by rogue political and commercial elements. Gelli was drawn to it in 1963, and with his CIA influence, quickly rose to the top. From there, he went on an aggressive recruitment drive, enlisting high-rank military contacts and leading business, political and criminal figures. When a targeted recruit was unwilling to join, Gelli inevitably turned to blackmail to force them to accept membership (he had access to the CIA files on everyone, so could pick the most embarrassing secrets as leverage).

As soon as Italian Freemasonry heard about the irregularities, the lodge was investigated and, with Decree 444LS, dated June 1976, disbanded. Gelli was expelled from Freemasonry. The change of status had no impact on him. He blithely ignored the fact that he was now running an illegal secret society as a rogue individual, and continued as he had before, using the P2 name and pretending a veneer of Masonry. In the meantime, the lodge continued to grow. Junior branches sprung up in many different locations, including in four different Latin American countries – Gelli often boasted of his friendship with General Juan Peron and the head of his death squads, José López Rega.

The Calvi Connection

A few years later, in March 1981, police raided his house in Arezzo. The documents they discovered in this operation included lists containing more than 900 names, among which was a number of very important civil servants, politicians, military officers, members of the secret service and leading business figures. Among the latter was Roberto Calvi, president of the Banco Ambrosiano of Milan – already in prison awaiting trial for the illegal export of capital. Other famous names from the lists included Silvio Berlusconi, who would go on to be the prime minister 20 years later, and Victor Emmanuel, the Prince of Naples.

The illegal lodge's activities were drawn into the public eye in 1982, after Calvi's Banco Ambrosiano collapsed. Calvi, known as God's Banker because of his links to the Vatican bank, was found dead. He'd been due

to give evidence about links between his bank, P2, the Mafia and the Vatican as part of an appeal, and for a week his disappearance was headline news. He was eventually found hanging under Blackfriars Bridge in London, and police announced that his death was suicide – after all, his bank, the largest in Italy, had collapsed, he had already received one four-year sentence, and he was in the dock on charges of alleged fraud.

In 2003 forensic scientists concluded that Calvi's death had been murder. The banker was escorted to the Thames river. Bruises on his arms and right wrist and marks on the soles of his shoes suggest that he fought when he was attacked – either on the edge of the river, or on a boat as it approached Blackfriars Bridge. After he was subdued, the team of killers applied "a slow, steady pressure", strangling him to the point of unconsciousness. The attackers then stuffed bricks into his pockets and down the front of his trousers, together with a large amount of cash. Calvi was still alive – but probably unconscious – when a noose was placed around his neck and an orange rope tied to a ring on scaffolding under the bridge. It was shortly after midnight on June 18, 1982. The killers then moved the boat away and the weight of the body and the bricks, combined with the river's current, tightened the noose. With water swirling around his legs, halfway up his calves, Calvi took anything from 30 to 60 minutes to die.

Despite the odd circumstances, even a verdict of suicide was enough to call Calvi's connections to Licio Gelli into focus. The press got hold of details about the lodge that police had been keeping secret.

Political Purposes

Among the lists and other documents it was revealed that police had also found a manifesto entitled *Piano di Rinascita Democratica* – "The Plan for Democratic Rebirth" – which described Gelli's objectives for the lodge: the formation of a new political and economic elite that would lead Italy away from democracy and back toward a more authoritarian form of government with decidedly fascist overtones. Shocked commentators described P2 as "a state within a state", horrified at its attempts to take over.

The scandal shattered the always-weak government. The prime minister at the time, Arnaldo Forlani, was eventually forced to resign. The lodge was then examined by a special commission of the Italian parliament, directed by Tina Anselmi of the Christian Democrat party. The conclusion of the commission was that it was an illegal, secret, criminal organization, even if no proof was found of specific crimes it committed. Gelli himself was finally acquitted of plotting to overthrow the Italian government and he was convicted to a dozen years in prison on a range of lesser charges. He fled into hiding after the Supreme Court upheld his sentence, and was eventually caught 17 years later, aged 79, in Cannes.

Most people are hazy when it comes to the overall facts of the story. The common perception is that there was a financial scandal, some ritual murders, a great deal of embezzlement, and that "the Freemasons" (worldwide, presumably) were behind it all. The truth is that Gelli was just yet another criminal with delusions of grandeur engaged in a perfectly everyday murderous embezzlement scheme, and that Freemasons were no more behind it than the CIA.

The Morgan Affair

The other major Masonic scandal – there are only two of any prominence, which is not bad going for 300 years – is the death of William Morgan in 1827. A Virginian, Morgan ran a successful distillery in Canada until 1823, when a fire destroyed his business and he was ruined. He moved to New York, and although it has been confirmed that he attained the Royal Arch Degree at a meeting in LeRoy, NY in 1825, it is also known that he was refused admission to both Blue Lodge and Royal Arch Chapter in his new home of Batavia, NY in 1823. There is no record of where (or even whether) he was initiated into Blue Lodge Masonry. When a new Chapter of the Royal Arch was proposed for Batavia, Morgan signed the petition. However, there were objections to his involvement again and a new petition was drawn up.

After this latest snub, Morgan became bitter and vengeful. He joined forces with David Miller, the editor of the local newspaper, who had been initiated as an Entered Apprentice, but subsequently thrown out of Masonry. Together, the two worked to defame the local Freemasons, both collectively and individually.

A classic anti-Masonry engraving depicting Freemasonry as the Antichrist, with beast at its feet.

The plan caused a lot of bad feeling, much of it against Morgan and Miller. The two became victims of ongoing harassment campaigns themselves. The newspaper's offices were set on fire to little effect. Although there are some questions as to whom was responsible, three local Masons were sent to jail for a time. In the meantime, Morgan was arrested repeatedly, sometimes for genuine wrong-doing, other times apparently on spurious charges. After yet another arrest, an anonymous man paid Morgan's bail, and left with him. Neither was ever seen again. Afterwards, a wide range of eyewitness reports surfaced, claiming everything from Morgan being given a wagon and allowed to ride off, to Morgan being grabbed by a gang of men and marched off.

A month or so later, a decomposing corpse was found some way outside of town. Morgan's (assumed) widow emphatically denied that it was her husband, on the basis of height, hair and so on. She changed her mind later, though, and said it was him. Another woman, named

Mrs Monroe, also claimed the corpse as her husband. Tales later filtered back about Morgan cropping up all over the world – a bit like Lord Lucan.

However, by far the most persistent theory at the time was that Morgan had been murdered by Freemasons. He became a cause with which populist politicians could beat the more successful members of society. Despite immediate condemnation from Freemasons at all levels regarding anyone who would kill Morgan, the American people were swept into a period of anti-Masonic fervour. Even now, his name is still used as proof of the murderous, satanic nature of Freemasonry. Nobody ever managed to solve the mystery or provide any clear proof for any of the various theories. Morgan's widow, curiously, went on to become one of the many wives of Mormon founder (and Freemason) Joseph Smith.

Dishonourable Mentions

Most Masonic detractors operate on the level of general hearsay and assumption – the "Oooh, my brother says they give each other all the best jobs, which is why he can't get promoted" brand of criticism, despite the fact that gratuitous nepotism can be enough to get a Mason into serious trouble with the lodge. However, there are a few individuals who are regularly held up by particularly well-researched Masonic detractors as examples of Freemasonry's villainy.

Ben "The Traitor" Arnold, persuading a subordinate to hide the fateful orders in a boot.

Benedict Arnold

In the USA, one of the better known is Ben Arnold, also known as "The Traitor". An officer in the American revolution as well as a Mason, Benedict Arnold was on the receiving end of all manner of political infighting during his career, and he eventually decided – when faced with comparatively pointless orders that would cost many, many lives – that the authorities were wrong. He did the unthinkable, and disobeyed, undoubtedly sparing many lives, but costing the revolutionaries their objective. He has been the subject of intense loathing in the USA ever since – a traitor is, after all, a traitor. By comparison, the Canadians consider him a hero, and he is utterly unknown in Britain and Australia.

Paul Bernardo

A convicted serial rapist from Toronto, currently serving a long jail sentence, Paul Bernardo was also at some point a Mason under Ontario's Grand Lodge, although he was thrown out. The dates of his stay in Masonry remain uncertain, so it's impossible to tell if he was an active Mason at the time he committed some of his atrocities. Only the most scurrilous of detractors attempt to suggest any sort of causal link between his crimes and the Craft.

Wilbur Mills

Finally, Arkansas congressman and Freemason Wilbur Mills was drummed out of the House of Representatives in the 1970s after he was found romping drunkenly in the "Tidal Basin" fountain with a stripper (one "Fannie Fox") in the middle of Washington DC. A one-time presidential hopeful, Mills later admitted long-term alcoholism and entered rehab. He eventually beat the disease and resumed his Masonic activities, if not his congressional ones.

Jim Davidson

Jim Davidson, outside Freemason's Hall in London, is a tireless and devoted charity campaigner.

British TV funny man Jim Davidson was forced to resign as Worshipful Master of Chelsea Lodge in London during 2002 – for performing exactly the sort of act that brought him to fame. Apparently, the off-colour routine offended a number of elderly attendees, who later wrote to complain to UGLE. There were no complaints on the night. Davidson offered apologies with his resignation, but seemed more fed up than apologetic, noting that he has always had complaints for his shows. The only mystery, really, is exactly what the gala attendees had expected from the famously "blue" comic. In real life, Davidson is known as a thoughtful, generous man who puts huge amounts of his personal time into charitable activities, particularly on behalf of supporting active soldiers in difficult situations. This particular "scandal" is really more of an indictment of the gala attendees than of the comic himself.

The Complete Revelations

Gabriel Jogand-Pages was born in Marseilles, France, in 1854. He received a good education and, on attaining his majority, decided on a career in journalism. His scorn for religious belief was equalled only by his general lack of a sense of decency. He was a talented writer, however, and the audacity of his work attracted a lot of attention. He quickly moved up to Paris, where he published a scandalous daily paper and wrote many successful, rather sacrilegious books – including *The Secret Lovers of Pope Pius IX*, for which he was heftily fined. In 1881, he was accepted as an Entered Apprentice, but didn't last long; his indiscretions were just too indiscreet.

In 1885, spotting an opportunity, Jogand-Pages pretended to see the light, and converted to Catholicism. He suppressed his offensive books, stopped attacking the church, and was absolved by the Roman Catholic Church. Noting the church's fanatical hatred of Masonry at the time, he then began a long period during which he produced a series of books called *The Complete Revelations of French Masonry*, written under the pseudonym Leo Taxil. They were great successes, and even saw translation into German, Italian and Spanish.

"Taxil" turned the full power of his ingenuity, irreverence and imagination to the *Complete Revelations*.

With a total disregard for anything resembling facts or research, he invented incredible layers of detail regarding the rites of the Craft – and their supposedly satanic nature. He swiftly painted the whole Craft as a particularly horrible type of devil worship. Volumes of the *Complete Revelations* were churned out on an almost monthly basis, each looking at different aspects of the "horror" of Masonry. Female Masons were the topic of a particularly salacious and lewd volume. Another – which sold more than 200,000 copies – gave spectacular detail regarding the way that every Mason became a murderer during his initiation, in spirit at least:

"Before a man may be admitted to a higher degree, he is blindfolded and led into a room where a live sheep is lying on the floor. The animal's mouth and feet are tied and it is cleanly shaven, so that it skin feels approximately like that of a person. Past the animal, a fellow brother stands, panting and pretending to struggle against several enemies. The blindfolded candidate is made to understand

Leo Taxil's "revelations" portrayed Freemasonry as a Judaic hotbed of Satanism, illustrated here in an engraving by A. Esnault.

Taxil painted Masonic initiations as particularly lurid and unbelievable, as exampled in this etching of a blindfolded initiate.

A witch helps a naked Freemason to see the future in a bowl of water in this eighteenth-century image, attributed to the Comte de Saint-Germain (*c*.1710–84).

that the sheep is a disloyal Mason who gave away the secrets of the order and now must die according to the ancient laws. The candidate is made executioner, as a warning to him. Then he is given a big knife, and after some ceremonial, is persuaded to kill the traitor – that is, to plunge the knife repeatedly into the body of the sheep, which he imagines to be that of an unknown human being, his Masonic brother. Thus every Mason is a murderer in spirit at least, if not in fact, for sometimes treacherous Masons are put in place of the animal."

The book, of course, drew horrified denials from Freemasons everywhere, including Otto von Bismarck, Emperor William I and the Prince of Wales, all of whom served to push its sales figures through the roof. The Vatican was said to be delighted at the series, and to read each instalment with great relish, as the books totally

vindicated their stance. Heartened by the sales figures and the public credulity, Taxil went on to push the envelope as hard as he could. He added spiritualism to his revelations, and described floating tables transforming into crocodiles under Satan's power. Pope Leo XIII was so pleased that he awarded Taxil the Order of the Holy Sepulchre.

The Satanic Heart

Meanwhile, the revelations continued. Taxil explained that the Satanic Heart of Masonry was the city of Charleston in South Carolina, home of Albert Pike, who had long worked tirelessly at perfecting the Scottish Rite. Taxil announced that in the Scottish Rite Consistory at Charleston, Lucifer regularly arrived and showed himself in all his glory – hooves, tail, red skin, huge phallus, the works. Realizing that an accommodating high priestess was aesthetically necessary for this conjuration, Taxil invented her – one "Diana Vaughn". Vaughn was said to be the direct descendant of the Babylonian goddess Astarte, and to have sworn herself to be the bride of the demon Asmodeus when still a little child. She was consecrated as Satan's own Masonic high priestess by the Lord of Lies, with the assistance of Albert Pike himself. She possessed diverse magical powers, including the ability to walk through walls, and to turn herself into a mobile pool of blood.

After several volumes of further implausible bosh, Taxil decided that Diana Vaughn should be converted, as he had been. This change of heart seems to have failed to provoke suspicion, having been supposedly prompted by Albert Pike's orders to spit on a host wafer and then stab it as part of a Masonic rite. Diana then wrote an exposé of her own, a copy of which was sent to the pope in 1895. Leo XIII had his secretary reply, thanking her, and urging her to continue her good work. Its tone and contents were naturally very similar to the Taxil documents, describing all manner of wonders, including choirs of deflowered children and a human-faced goat that spoke evil incantations.

Eventually, in 1896, the pope organized an anti-Masonic congress in Austria, where Masonic lodges were prohibited at the time. A thousand delegates attended from all around Europe, including 36 Roman Catholic bishops. Taxil was the hero of the event, but he found himself under pressure to introduce Diana Vaughn. His plausible excuses did not entirely satisfy the group, and finally he had to announce that he would introduce her to the world in Paris on Easter Monday, 1897.

A large audience assembled to meet the devil's former lover, and at the appointed time, Taxil took the stage. He then told his shocked and horrified audience that he was and always had been Jogand-Page, that his conversion had been a lie, that Vaughn was a literary creation, that every single word of his *Complete Revelations* was an utter lie. Furthermore, he said that he had done it all for the sole purpose of exposing the idiotic gullibility of the Catholic Church and its rulers, and showing intelligent men everywhere how ridiculous it all was. He confirmed that the Bishop of Charleston had informed the pope that the stories were complete rubbish, and that the pope had said nothing. Jogand-Page had to be rushed from the conference under police protection and hidden in a different quarter of the city.

The church reacted with predictable scorn and disgust regarding the whole matter. Later in an interview, Jogand-Page said of the Taxil work:

"The public made me what I am, the arch-liar of the period, for when I first commenced to write against the Masons my object was amusement, pure and simple. The crimes laid at their door were so grotesque, so impossible, so widely exaggerated, I thought everybody would see the joke and give me credit for originating a new line of humour. But my readers wouldn't have it so; they accepted my fables as gospel truth, and the more I lied for the purpose of showing that I lied, the more convinced became they that I was a paragon of veracity."

Every so often, the Taxil accusations resurface as part of some poor fool's ill-advised attacks against Masonry – but at least they provide a quick way to identify the lunatic fringe of Masonic antagonists.

The State of the Craft

The world has changed a lot in the last 60 years. The social realities that we took for granted in the 1950s have become fond memories and pipe dreams. The structure of life itself has shifted sharply, and not for the better. At the same time, Freemasonry's membership has plummeted. The new world needs Freemasonry and its lessons more than ever before, but can the Craft adapt enough to carry the word forward for even another decade? That remains to be seen.

The 1950s and 60s are remembered across the West as golden decades by those fortunate enough to have lived through them. The trials and hardships of the Second World War were finished. Reconstruction and new development meant that the economy was booming. The rich were rich and the poor were poor, but the difference between the two was a lot less, and only a tiny fraction of the available money had been sucked up into the top 0.1 per cent of the population. Doors were often left unlocked, children were allowed to just "go out and play", and when a teenager was late home, it was fear of scandal and pregnancy that kept parents awake.

A family could afford to live on one wage, even a national average one. Workers knew that their jobs had a career attached, that their pensions would provide for their old age, that their mortgages would pay for their homes, and that as long as they did their part diligently their lives would be fairly comfortable. For the ambitious and talented, it was even better; there were plenty of opportunities for hard work and skill to find rich rewards. A good percentage of the population could aspire to enough wealth for a car and a couple of holidays every year, a good education for the kids, and enough put by to keep life manageable into old age. Corporations competed vigorously, but with decorum, desperate to avoid causing the sort of scandal that would harm their share price. Outside of work and family life, there wasn't all that much to do – entertainment was not that big a deal.

Life, in short, was comfortable. Right across the English-speaking world (and more besides), there was a feeling that we'd got it right at last, that things were going to be good for a while, and that progress would only make things better. Just as long as the cold war stayed cold, we'd be able to solve the world's problems somehow, find a way to bring everyone else up to the same level.

But the shift had already started. Greed is insidious. This is demonstrated by a famous piece of psychological game theory called "Hawks and Doves", in which doves represent cooperation (fair play), and

African-American Freemasons parade through the streets of 1950s' New Orleans, Louisiana.

The Spirit of Equality – shown holding the 1789 French "Declaration of Human Rights and of the Citizen" – is at the heart of Masonry. Note the Masonic symbols bordering the image.

hawks represent exploitation (greed). The simplest version simply pits hawks against doves at different percentages of each, and tracks how the overall population scores. When two doves meet, both win a little. When a hawk and a dove meet, the hawk wins big, and the dove loses big. Finally, when two hawks meet, both lose a little. If the great majority of players are doves, then the few hawks make an absolute killing, but everyone does all right. As the number of hawks increases, the overall score goes down, and only a small percentage of hawks do well. Finally, when the game is mostly hawks, everyone loses massively (but the few doves get totally slaughtered).

The game can get a lot more complex – with resource exploitation, breeding and dying cycles, retaliator strategies and so on – but if breeding is introduced, then the hawk population tends to wipe out the dove population, unless the cost of hawk versus hawk conflict is set high.

The parallels to the changes in our society are pretty clear, frankly. Fifty years down the line, jobs are lucky to last three years, even high-end workers need two salaries to pay for a family, working hours and stress levels are through the roof, parents dare not let their children out of their sight let alone allow them to play all day unsupervised, divorce rates are rocketing, pensions are starting to look like a hollow joke, corporations have lost all sense of decency, shame and sanity, and the money has been so concentrated at the "top" of society that it's a wonder anyone has any left at all.

New World Order

In 2001, the top 5 per cent richest people in the USA held an amazing 59 per cent of the money in the country –

A chilling psychological model, the game "Hawks and Doves" shows how antisocial behaviour spreads until society collapses.

33 per cent of it with the top 1 per cent. That's just 41 per cent of the cash across the 95 per cent of the population; worse still, about 2 per cent of the cash was distributed across the bottom 50 per cent. These figures get worse every year, too, as the top 5 per cent take home more money than the bottom 50 per cent put together. It's not the way it always was, either; between 1947 and 1974, the average increase in earnings per family was around 100 per cent, right across society. A little more in the bottom 20 per cent, and a little less in the top 20 per cent, but pretty consistent. Between 1974 and 1998, the amount of money ("real" – in other words, the actual number of dollars) earned by the bottom 20 per cent increased by just 3 per cent, while it increased by nearly 90 per cent for the top 20 per cent – and they were earning something like five times as much to begin with, even before you take their vast savings into account.

Ken Patterson, Assistant Grand Master of the Grand Lodge of Ireland, welcoming the public in to look around in 2000.

The USA is the most extreme example of a rich–poor divide, but the UK, Canada, Australia and Europe are just a cat's whisker behind it . . . and taken globally, of course, the figures are much, much worse. But just think about those figures for a second, and what they imply. Is it any wonder things have got hard, and are getting harder? How many doves are left, before meltdown?

As our quality of life charges down the toilet, we're filling the gap with reams of new options for entertainment – anything to take the pressure off for a while, help numb the stress and pain. Time is in short supply, though; poorer standards of life mean longer hours worked, and yet more time involved in organizing life. Even before television, movies, the Internet and video games, there's just not much free time left for relaxation any more.

Membership Today

Faced with this brave new world, Freemasonry is having great trouble competing. It asks its members for time on a fairly regular basis. It takes work to prepare for meetings. There are fees to be paid: to the lodge, and for dining. Frankly, it is becoming a luxury that fewer and fewer can manage.

The statistics are shocking and remarkably consistent worldwide. From a peak membership in the 1960s – up to 3.6 million US members in 1966 – Freemasonry has shrunk by more than 50 per cent (1.6 million US members in 2002). As it has shrunk, its average age has increased. In the 1950s, the average age of a Freemason was around 40 years. Now, it's just a little under 70 years. The Craft is dying of old age, and it is happening quickly – in addition, the venerable members just don't have as much energy or capacity to make changes as younger members do. Worse still, attendance rates have dropped from an average of 60 per cent or more to around 10 per cent; in other words, the number of active Masons has gone from about 2 million in the USA to about 150,000 – a drop of 92.5 per cent. The most worrying statistic of all is that most new members – as many as 90 per cent – stay long enough to get to Master Mason and then just drop out.

In 1988, a professional public survey company was hired to find out what non-Masons knew about the

Even in 1992, UGLE's Annual General Meeting showed its members' advancing average age.

Craft, and how they felt about possible membership. The results were certainly indicative of Freemasonry's problems. At the time, only 15 per cent of men belonged to some sort of organization, and most said that they lacked the time to do anything of that sort; 56 per cent estimated that they had just 1 hour a week spare. Only 2 per cent of the survey were actively interested in membership, but a further 22 per cent said they would consider it if the benefits were good enough.

When asked for details, the top benefits of that sort of society were considered to be (in order): meeting new friends, doing community work, engaging in social activity, doing things with current friends, doing things with family, making professional contacts, developing leadership skills and, lastly, taking a leadership position. As for the society's reputation, 71 per cent had no idea what it was, and 26 per cent claimed a rough idea and a

favourable impression. Only 3 per cent of the population surveyed claimed to have a neutral or negative opinion of the society.

A year later, the same team was called back to research the Masonic membership itself. At that time, 1989, the team found that 53 per cent of the members were over 60 years – a figure that is now considerably higher. Almost two-thirds had been Masons for more than 20 years, and 95 per cent of those members had stopped attending the lodge even occasionally. Less than a third had gone beyond the Symbolic Lodge. Overall, a total of 87 per cent of the membership said that they were perfectly satisfied with Freemasonry, but they did not attend. Three-quarters of them said that this was because of time considerations, but two-thirds who said so were retired, and three-quarters of them were not involved with any other organization.

A German lodge carpet, c.1760, called an "Arbeitsteppich", shows the magnificent symbolism of the Craft. Freemasonry's rich mysteries need defending and re-expressing in the modern world.

Declining Interest in the Craft

The conclusions are fairly inescapable. Most of the membership, worldwide, is sitting at home happy with the way things are and disinterested in change, yet not motivated enough to actually attend a meeting. Meanwhile, the potential new recruits value family, community, charity, fellowship and leadership, but have very little time, and know next to nothing about the Craft. Between the two, membership levels are collapsing and the members themselves are getting older and older.

The Future of Freemasonry

There are obviously underlying problems. After six months' membership, only 15 per cent of new recruits bother attending meetings; and that continues falling to just 5 per cent of long-term members. That has to mean that the lodges are either not fulfilling members' needs or that they are not interesting enough to drag people away from their usual activities. Given that the majority of members are retired, it is not as if most of them have put in a hard day's work beforehand. As we have seen in this book, Freemasonry is a vibrant, symbol-rich mystery tradition with some vitally important lessons – even more important today, in our new, hostile world,

than ever before. There must be some gulf between the content of Freemasonry and its experience.

It has been suggested that most lodge meetings are repetitive, with the same rituals and orders of business time after time. On top of that, being a lodge officer requires huge amounts of work memorizing vast tracts of text, and in many lodges, a certain amount of study is required before a member can be raised to Master Mason. The pay-offs, obviously, are not good enough in these stressful times. The 1988 survey made perfectly clear what people want from the Craft. They are all things that are perfectly manageable within the current constitutions. It seems that Freemasonry as a whole needs to take a long, hard look at how it can deliver the things that members want from it if it's going to survive into the future.

Simply doing what has been done before is not enough. The world is very different, today. The old ways no longer work. Freemasonry must adapt itself, and it must do it right now. If it fails, the shining heart of the Enlightenment – the last great Western mystery school – will wither and die, choked in old age, apathy and dust. And in a time that needs its teachings more than ever, that would be a crime beyond redemption.

An old room of reflection encourages would-be Masons to contemplate the meaning of their lives.

Former UGLE Senior Grand Deacon, John Hamill, opens the Grand Temple doors in 2002 to help dispel perceptions of elitism.

APPENDIX

Grand Lodges for selected territories worldwide. For each listed territory, the Grand Lodge responsible for the Symbolic/Blue Lodges in that area, for each jurisdiction, where appropriate is listed, with websites and/or email addresses where available ("ncd" is used to indicate "no contact details"). In each area, the first lodge listed is considered the area's primary regular Grand Lodge. Please note that there is not room in this work for a complete list; there are many more Grand Lodges densely packed across Europe, Central and Southern America, and also some more lightly distributed across Africa and Asia. For a complete list of all Grand Lodges known worldwide – regular or otherwise – please visit Paul Bessel's superb and extensive website at http://bessel.org/gls.htm.

AUSTRALIA AND NEW ZEALAND

New South Wales: United Grand Lodge of New South Wales and Australian Capital Territory, http://www.uglnsw.freemasonry.org.au. Le Droit Humain (mixed-sex, "irregular"), http://www.australianco-masonry.netfirms.com, email megk@iprimus.com.au.

New Zealand: Grand Lodge of New Zealand, http://www.freemasons.co.nz.

Northern Territory: *see* South Australia.

Queensland: United Grand Lodge of Queensland, http://www.uglq.org.au. Le Droit Humain, http://www.australianco-masonry.netfirms.com, email HowardSmith60@bigpond.com.au.

South Australia: Grand Lodge of South Australia and the Northern Territory, http://www.freemasonrysaust.org.au. Le Droit Humain, http://www.australianco-masonry.netfirms.com, email lboath@pembroke.sa.edu.au.

Tasmania: Grand Lodge of Tasmania, Ancient Free and Accepted Masons, http://www.freemasonrytasmania.org.

Victoria: United Grand Lodge of Victoria, http://www.freemasonscis.net.au. Le Droit Humain, http://www.australianco-masonry.netfirms.com, email lephils@alphalink.com.au.

Western Australia: Grand Lodge of Western Australia, http://www.gl-of-wa.org.au. Le Droit Humain, http://www.australianco-masonry.netfirms.com, email kleyn@iprimus.com.au.

CANADA

Alberta: Grand Lodge of Alberta, http://www.freemasons.ab.ca. Most Worshipful Prince Hall Grand Lodge of Alberta, ncd.

British Columbia: Grand Lodge of British Columbia and Yukon, http://www.freemasonry.bcy.ca. Most Worshipful Prince Hall Grand Lodge Free and Accepted Masons Washington and Jurisdiction (USA), http://www.mwphglwa.org. Le Droit Humaine, http://www.dhcanada.org, email illumination@dhcanada.org.

Labrador: *see* Newfoundland.

Manitoba: Grand Lodge of Manitoba, http://members.home.net/bobgalbr. Most Worshipful Prince Hall Grand Lodge of Minnesota and Jurisdiction (USA), tel. +1 612 824 5150.

New Brunswick: Grand Lodge of New Brunswick, http://www.glnb.ca.

Newfoundland: Grand Lodge of Newfoundland and Labrador, http://www.newcomm.net/masonic.

Nova Scotia: Grand Lodge of Nova Scotia, http://www.grandlodgens.org.

Ontario: Grand Lodge of Canada in the Province of Ontario, http://grandlodge.on.ca. Most Worshipful Prince Hall Grand Lodge Free and Accepted Masons of the Province of Ontario and Jurisdiction, ncd.

Prince Edward Island: Grand Lodge of Prince Edward Island, http://www.freemasonry.pe.ca. Most Worshipful Prince Hall Grand Lodge Free and Accepted Masons of the Province of Ontario and Jurisdiction, ncd.

Quebec: Grand Lodge of Quebec, http://glq.cedep.net. Most Worshipful Prince Hall Grand Lodge Free and Accepted Masons of the Province of Ontario and Jurisdiction, ncd. Le Droit Humaine, http://www.dhcanada.org, email liberte@dhcanada.org. Grand Orient d'France (continental juris.), http://www.godf.org/english/index_k.htm. Grand Loge d'France (anglo juris.), http://www.gldf.org/html/content.htm. National Grand Lodge of Canada (mixed-sex, irregular), http://www.glnc.org/englindex.htm.

Saskatchewan: Grand Lodge of Saskatchewan, http://masons.sk.ca.

GREAT BRITAIN AND IRELAND

England: United Grand Lodge of England, http://www.ugle.co.uk. The Honourable Fraternity of Ancient Freemasons (women only), http://www.powerpro.demon.co.uk/hfaf. The Order of Women Freemasons (women only), tel. +44 171 229 2368. International Co-Freemasonry (mixed sex), tel. +44 181 339 9000. Le Droit Humain, http://www.droit-humain.org/uk.

Ireland (all): Grand Lodge of Ireland, http://www.irish-freemasons.org. Le Droit Humain, http://www.droit-humain.org.

Scotland: Grand Lodge of Scotland, http://www.grandlodgescotland.com. Le Droit Humain, http://www.droit-humain.org/uk.

Wales: United Grand Lodge of England, http://www.ugle.co.uk.

SOUTH AFRICA

South Africa: Grand Lodge of South Africa, http://www.grandlodge.co.za/glsamain.html.

UNITED STATES OF AMERICA

Alabama: Grand Lodge Free and Accepted Masons of Alabama, http://www.alagl.org, email gsec@alagl.org. Most Worshipful Prince Hall Grand Lodge Free and Accepted Masons of Alabama, tel. +1 205 328 9078. Progressive Free and Accepted Masons of the USA (irregular), ncd. American Federation of Human Rights (mixed, irregular), http://www.co-masonry.org. Le Droit Humain American Federation (mixed), http://www.comasonic.org.

Alaska: Grand Lodge of Free and Accepted Masons of Alaska, http://www.alaska-mason.org, email grandlodge@alaska.com. Most Worshipful Prince Hall Grand Lodge Free and Accepted Masons Alaska and its Jurisdiction, Inc., tel. +1 907 646 2210. Most Worshipful King Solomon Grand Lodge Ancient Free and Accepted Masons, Inc. (irregular), ncd. American Federation of Human Rights (mixed, irregular), http://www.co-masonry.org. Le Droit Humain American Federation (mixed), http://www.comasonic.org.

Arizona: Grand Lodge of Arizona Free and Accepted Masons, http://www.azmasons.org, email azgnd_ldg@azmasons.org. Most Worshipful Prince Hall Grand Lodge Free and Accepted Masons Arizona and Jurisdiction, Inc., http://www.azmwphgl.com. Ezra Grand Lodge Ancient Free and Accepted Masons (irregular), ncd. American Federation of Human Rights (mixed, irregular), http://www.co-masonry.org. Le Droit Humain American Federation (mixed), http://www.comasonic.org.

Arkansas: Most Worshipful Grand Lodge Free and Accepted Masons of Arkansas, http://www.arkmason.org, email jlweatherall@juno.com. Most Worshipful Prince Hall Grand Lodge Free and Accepted Masons, Inc., Jurisdiction of Arkansas, http://arkphagrandlodge.com. St. James Grand Lodge Ancient Free and Accepted Masons (irregular), ncd. American Federation of Human Rights (mixed, irregular), http://www.co-masonry.org. Le Droit Humain American Federation (mixed), http://www.comasonic.org.

California: Grand Lodge Free and Accepted Masons of California, http://www.freemason.org, email gloffice@freemason.org. Most Worshipful Prince Hall Grand Lodge, Free and Accepted Masons, State of California, Inc., http://mwphglch.org. Most Worshipful Golden Gate Grand Lodge Ancient Free and Accepted Masons (irregular), ncd. Esoteric Grand Lodge of America (irregular), ncd. American Federation of Human Rights (mixed, irregular), http://www.co-masonry.org. Le Droit Humain American Federation (mixed), http://www.comasonic.org. Grand Orient de France, http://www.godf.org/foreign/uk/index_uk.html. Women's Grand Lodge of Belgium (women only), http://users.swing.be/mason/index_en.htm.

Colorado: Most Worshipful Grand Lodge of Ancient Free and Accepted Masons of Colorado, http://www.coloradomasons.org, email gloffice@coloradomasons.org. Most Worshipful Prince Hall Grand Lodge of Colorado, Wyoming, Utah and Parts of South Korea, http://www.users.uswest.net/~rfharlan. Ivanhoe Grand Lodge, Ancient Free and Accepted Masons (irregular), ncd. American Federation of Human Rights (mixed, irregular), http://www.co-masonry.org. Le Droit Humain American Federation (mixed), http://www.comasonic.org.

Connecticut: Grand Lodge of Connecticut Ancient Free and Accepted Masons, http://www.ctfreemasons.net, email grandlodge@masonicare.org. Most Worshipful Prince Hall Grand Lodge of Connecticut, Inc., Free and Accepted Masons, tel. +1 203 329 9957. St. John's Grand Lodge, Ancient Free and Accepted Masons (irregular), ncd. American Federation of Human Rights (mixed, irregular), http://www.co-masonry.org. Le Droit Humain American Federation (mixed), http://www.comasonic.org.

Delaware: Grand Lodge of Ancient Free and Accepted Masons of Delaware, http://www.masonsindelaware.org, email grandsecdel@masonsindelaware.org. Most Worshipful Prince Hall Grand Lodge Free and Accepted Masons of Delaware, http://mwphgl-de.s5.com. International Free and Accepted Masons (irregular), ncd. American Federation of Human Rights (mixed, irregular), http://www.co-masonry.org. Le Droit Humain American Federation (mixed), http://www.comasonic.org.

District of Columbia: Grand Lodge Free Ancient and Accepted Masons of the District of Columbia, http://dcgrandlodge.org, grandlodge@dcgrandlodge.org. Most Worshipful Prince Hall Grand Lodge, Free and Accepted Masons, PHA, Jurisdiction of the District of Columbia, Inc., http://mwphgldc.com. George Washington Union (mixed), http://www.chez.com/gwu. Women's Grand Lodge of Belgium (female), http://users.swing.be/mason/index_en.htm. Huge B. Ings Grand Lodge (irregular), ncd. American Federation of Human Rights (mixed, irregular), http://www.co-masonry.org. Le Droit Humain American Federation (mixed), http://www.comasonic.org.

Florida: Most Worshipful Grand Lodge of Free and Accepted Masons of Florida, http://www.glflamason.org, email gsoffice@glflamason.org. Most Worshipful Union Grand Lodge, Free and Accepted Masons, Prince Hall Affiliated, Florida and Belize, Central America Jurisdiction, Inc., http://www.mwuglflorida.org. Meridian Grand Lodge (irregular), ncd. American Federation of Human Rights (mixed, irregular), http://www.co-masonry.org. Le Droit Humain American Federation (mixed), http://www.comasonic.org.

Georgia: Grand Lodge of Free and Accepted Masons for the State of Georgia, http://www.glofga.org, email fam2@bellsouth.net. Most Worshipful Prince Hall Grand Lodge Free and Accepted Masons Jurisdiction of Georgia, http://www.mwphgl-georgia.org. Travelling Masons of the World, Inc. (irregular), ncd. American Federation of Human Rights (mixed, irregular), http://www.co-masonry.org. Le Droit Humain American Federation (mixed), http://www.comasonic.org.

Hawaii: Grand Lodge of Hawaii Free and Accepted Masons, http://www.grandlodgehi.com, email grandsecretary@grandlodgehawaii.com. Most Worshipful Prince Hall Grand Lodge of Hawaii, http://www.mwphglofhawaii.org.

Idaho: Grand Lodge Ancient Free and Accepted Masons of Idaho, http://www.idahoaf.am. (Prince Hall Masonry, established by Grand Lodge of Oregon and Nevada.)

Illinois: Grand Lodge of Illinois Ancient Free and Accepted Masons, http://www.ilmason.org, email bobkalb@afam-il.org. Most Worshipful Prince Hall Grand Lodge Free and Accepted Masons State of Illinous and Jurisdiction, http://www.mwphglil.com. Hiram Grand Lodge (irregular), ncd. American Federation of Human Rights (mixed, irregular), http://www.co-masonry.org. Le Droit Humain American Federation (mixed), http://www.comasonic.org.

Indiana: Grand Lodge of Indiana Free and Accepted Masons, http://www.indianamasons.org, roger@indianamasons.org. Most Worshipful Prince Hall Grand Lodge Free and Accepted Masons of the Jurisdiction of Indiana, http://www.sigmaduke.com/glodgein. Most Worshipful KSS Grand Lodge of Indiana (irregular), ncd. American Federation of Human Rights (mixed, irregular), http://www.co-masonry.org. Le Droit Humain American Federation (mixed), http://www.comasonic.org.

Iowa: Grand Lodge of Iowa Ancient Free and Accepted Masons, http://www.gl-iowa.org, email gliowa@qwest.net. Most Worshipful Prince Hall Grand Lodge of Iowa and Jurisdiction, Inc., ncd. Daniel Grand Lodge (irregular), ncd. American Federation of Human Rights (mixed, irregular), http://www.co-masonry.org. Le Droit Humain American Federation (mixed), http://www.comasonic.org.

Kansas: Grand Lodge of Kansas Ancient Free and Accepted Masons, http://gl-ks.org, email glksafam@alltel.net. Most Worshipful Prince Hall Grand Lodge Free and Accepted Masons of Kansas and its Jurisdictions, http://www.phglks.org. American Federation of Human Rights (mixed, irregular), http://www.co-masonry.org. Le Droit Humain American Federation (mixed), http://www.comasonic.org.

Kentucky: Grand Lodge of Kentucky Free and Accepted Masons, http://grandlodgeofkentucky.org, email glofky@aol.com. Most Worshipful Prince Hall Grand Lodge Free and Accepted Masons of Kentucky, tel. +1 502 776 5560. Kings of Kentucky Grand Lodge (irregular), ncd. American Federation of Human Rights (mixed, irregular), http://www.co-masonry.org. Le Droit Humain American Federation (mixed), http://www.comasonic.org.

Louisiana: Grand Lodge of the State of Louisiana Free and Accepted Masons, http://www.la-mason.com/gl.htm, email glodge@cox-internet.com. Most Worshipful Prince Hall Grand Lodge Free and Accepted Masons for the State of Louisiana and Jurisdiction, http://www.theplumbline.org. General Grand Masonic Congress of Ancient Free and Accepted Masons of the United State of America (irregular), ncd. American Federation of Human Rights (mixed, irregular), http://www.co-masonry.org. Le Droit Humain American Federation (mixed), http://www.comasonic.org.

Maine: Grand Lodge of Maine Ancient Free and Accepted, http://www.mainemason.org, email grandlodge@mainemason.org. (Prince Hall Masonry, established by Grand Lodge of Massachusetts.)

Maryland: Grand Lodge of Ancient, Free and Accepted Masons of Maryland, http://www.mdmasons.org/gl/default.asp, email glmaryland@erols.com. Most Worshipful Prince Hall Grand Lodge of Free and Accepted Masons State of Maryland and Jurisdiction, http://www.mwphglmd.org. Harmony Grand Lodge in the Great State of Maryland (irregular), ncd. American Federation of Human Rights (mixed, irregular), http://www.co-masonry.org. Le Droit Humain American Federation (mixed), http://www.comasonic.org.

Massachusetts: Most Worshipful Grand Lodge of Ancient Free and Accepted Masons of the Commonwealth of Massachusetts, http://www.glmasons-mass.org, email grandsec@glmasons-mass.org. Prince Hall Grand Lodge Free and Accepted Masons Jurisdiction of Massachusetts, http://www.princehall.org. George Washington Carver Grand Lodge (irregular), ncd. American Federation of Human Rights (mixed, irregular), http://www.co-masonry.org. Le Droit Humain American Federation (mixed), http://www.comasonic.org.

Michigan: Grand Lodge of Michigan Free and Accepted Masons, http://www.gl-mi.org, email gl-office@gl-mi.org. Most Worshipful Prince Hall Grand Lodge Free and Accepted Masons Jurisdiction of Michigan, http://www.miphgl.org. International Free and Accepted Modern Masons and Order of Eastern Stars (irregular), ncd. American Federation of Human Rights (mixed, irregular), http://www.co-masonry.org. Le Droit Humain American Federation (mixed), http://www.comasonic.org.

Minnesota: Grand Lodge of Minnesota Ancient Free and Accepted Masons, http://mn-mason.org, email mn-mason@spacestar.com. Most Worshipful Prince Hall Grand Lodge of Minnesota and Jurisdiction, tel. +1 612 824 5150.

Mississippi: Grand Lodge of Mississippi Free and Accepted Masons, Mississippi, http://msgrandlodge.org, email grsec@msgrandlodge.org. Most Worshipful Stringer Grand Lodge Free and Accepted Masons (Prince Hall Affiliations) Jurisdiction of Mississippi, tel. +1 601 354 1403. Most Worshipful Prince Hall Grand Lodge Free and Accepted Masons of the Jurisdiction of Mississippi, ncd. American Federation of Human Rights (mixed, irregular), http://www.co-masonry.org. Le Droit Humain American Federation (mixed), http://www.comasonic.org.

Missouri: Grand Lodge of the Ancient Free and Accepted Masons, http://www.momason.org, email rmiller@tranquility.net. Most Worshipful Prince Hall Grand Lodge Free and Accepted Masons of Missouri and Jurisdiction, http://www.phaglmo. John A. Belle Grand Lodge of Missouri, Inc. (irregular), ncd. American Federation of Human Rights (mixed, irregular), http://www.co-masonry.org. Le Droit Humain American Federation (mixed), http://www.comasonic.org.

Montana: Montana Grand Lodge Ancient Free and Accepted Masons, http://www.grandlodgemontana.org, email mtglsec@grandlodgemontana.org. (Prince Hall Masonry, established by Grand Lodge of Oregon.)

Nebraska: Grand Lodge Ancient Free and Accepted Masons of Nebraska, http://www.nebraska-grand-lodge.org. Most Worshipful Prince Hall Grand Lodge Free and Accepted Masons of Nebraska and its Jurisdiction, http://mwphglne.org. American Federation of Human Rights (mixed, irregular), http://www.co-masonry.org. Le Droit Humain American Federation (mixed), http://www.comasonic.org.

Nevada: Grand Lodge of Free and Accepted Masons of the State of Nevada, http://www.nvmasons.org, email nvgsec@nvmasons.org. Most Worshipful Prince Hall Grand Lodge Free and Accepted Masons of Nevada, Inc., http://pw2.netcom.com/~cwsearcy/index1.htm. Rising Sun Grand Lodge (irregular), ncd. American Federation of Human Rights (mixed, irregular), http://www.co-masonry.org. Le Droit Humain American Federation (mixed), http://www.comasonic.org.

New Hampshire: Grand Lodge of New Hampshire Free and Accepted Masons, http://www.nhgrandlodge.org. (Prince Hall Masonry, established by Grand Lodge of Massachusetts.)

New Jersey: Grand Lodge of New Jersey Free and Accepted Masons, http://njfreemasonry.org, email gen_misc@njmasonic.org. Most Worshipful Prince Hall Grand Lodge Free and Accepted Masons State of New Jersey, http://www.mwphglnj.org. Garden State Grand Lodge Ancient Free and Accepted Masons (irregular), http://www.geocities.com/athens/delphi/6637. American Federation of Human Rights (mixed, irregular), http://www.co-masonry.org. Le Droit Humain American Federation (mixed), http://www.comasonic.org.

New Mexico: Grand Lodge of New Mexico Ancient Free and Accepted Masons, http://nmmasons.org, email nmgndldg@juno.com. Most Worshipful Prince Hall Grand Lodge Free and Accepted Masons of the State of New Mexico, Inc., http://www.mwphglnm.org. American Federation of Human Rights (mixed, irregular), http://www.co-masonry.org. Le Droit Humain American Federation (mixed), http://www.comasonic.org.

New York: Grand Lodge of New York Free and Accepted Masons, http://www.nymasons.org, email grand_secretary@nymasons.org. M.W. Prince Hall Grand Lodge of the Most Ancient and Honorable Fraternity of Free and Accepted Masons of the State of New York, http://www.geocities.com/mwphglony. American Federation of Human Rights (mixed, irregular), http://www.co-masonry.org. Le Droit Humain American Federation (mixed), http://www.comasonic.org. La Serenisima Gran Logia de Lengua Espanolo (Para Los EE UU de Norte America), http://www.msnr.org/usala. La Grande Lodge of Saint Jean of Orients, Inc. (irregular), ncd. Grand Lodge Symbolic of Memphis-Misraïm for the United State and its Jurisdictions Ancient and Primitive Rite of

Memphis-Misraïm (irregular), http://www.iss-ic-memphis-misraim.org. Grand Lodge Ancient Universal Mysteries (irregular), http://www.grandlodgeaum.org/index.html. Grand Orient de France, http://www.godf.org/foreign/uk/index_uk.html. Women's Grand Lodge of Belgium (women only), http://users.swing.be/mason/index_en.htm.

North Carolina: Grand Lodge of North Carolina Ancient Free and Accepted Masons, http://www.grandlodge-nc.org, email rcarter@grandlodge-nc.org. Most Worshipful Prince Hall Grand Lodge of Free and Accepted Masons of North Carolina and Jurisdictions, Inc., http://www.mwphglnc.com. Modern Free and Accepted Masons of the World (irregular), ncd. American Federation of Human Rights (mixed, irregular), http://www.co-masonry.org. Le Droit Humain American Federation (mixed), http://www.comasonic.org.

North Dakota: Grand Lodge of North Dakota Ancient Free and Accepted Masons, http://mastermason.com/glnd/glndindex.htm, email masonnd@aol.com. (Prince Hall Masonry car of Minnesota.)

Ohio: Grand Lodge of Ohio Free and Accepted Masons, http://www.freemason.com, email gbraatz@freemason.com. Most Worshipful Prince Hall Grand Lodge of Ohio Free and Accepted Masons, http://www.phaohio.org. International Grand Lodge of Masonic Brotherhood (irregular), ncd. American Federation of Human Rights (mixed, irregular), http://www.co-masonry.org. Le Droit Humain American Federation (mixed), http://www.comasonic.org.

Oklahoma: Grand Lodge of Oklahoma Ancient Free and Accepted Masons, http://www.gloklahoma.org. Most Worshipful Prince Hall Grand Lodge Free and Accepted Masons Jurisdiction of Oklahoma, http://www.geocities.com/okj_mwphgl. American Federation of Human Rights (mixed, irregular), http://www.co-masonry.org. Le Droit Humain American Federation (mixed), http://www.comasonic.org.

Oregon: Grand Lodge of Oregon Ancient Free and Accepted Masons, http://www.masonic-oregon.com, email grandsecretary@masonic-oregon.com. Most Worshipful Prince Hall Grand Lodge Free and Accepted Masons of Oregon, Inc., tel. +1 503 218 2225. American Federation of Human Rights (mixed, irregular), http://www.co-masonry.org. Le Droit Humain American Federation (mixed), http://www.comasonic.org.

Pennsylvania: Grand Lodge of Pennsylvania Free and Accepted Masons, http://www.pagrandlodge.org, email gsoffice@pagrandlodge.org. Most Worshipful Prince Hall Grand Lodge of Pennsylvania Free and Accepted Masons, http://www.princehall-pa.org. American Federation of Human Rights (mixed, irregular), http://www.co-masonry.org. Le Droit Humain American Federation (mixed), http://www.comasonic.org.

Rhode Island: Grand Lodge of Rhode Island Free and Accepted Masons, http://www.rimasons.org, email grandlodge@rimasons.org. Most Worshipful Prince Hall Grand Lodge Free and Accepted Masons of the State of Rhode Island, tel. +1 401 461 2600.

South Carolina: Grand Lodge of South Carolina Ancient Free Masons, http://www.scgrandlodgeafm.org, email scgrandlodge@juno.com. Most Worshipful Prince Hall Grand Lodge of Free and Accepted Masons of the State of South Carolina, http://www.mwphglsc.org. New Hope Grand Lodge (irregular), ncd. American Federation of Human Rights (mixed, irregular), http://www.co-masonry.org. Le Droit Humain American Federation (mixed), http://www.comasonic.org.

South Dakota: Grand Lodge of South Dakota Ancient Free and Accepted Masons, http://mastermason.com/southdakota, email glodgeofsd@ll.net. (Prince Hall Masonry, established by Grand Lodge of Kansas.)

Tennessee: Grand Lodge of Tennessee Free and Accepted Masons, http://www.grandlodge-tn.org, email grsectn@korrnet.org. Most Worshipful Prince Hall Grand Lodge Free and Accepted Masons of Tennessee, tel. +1 901 774 7230. Travelling Masons of the World, Inc. (irregular), ncd. American Federation of Human Rights (mixed, irregular), http://www.co-masonry.org. Le Droit Humain American Federation (mixed), http://www.comasonic.org.

Texas: Grand Lodge of Texas Ancient Free and Accepted Masons, http://www.grandlodgeoftexas.org. Prince Hall Grand Lodge of Texas, http://www.mwphglotx.org. Grand Lodge of Deliberation of Texas (irregular), ncd. Federation of Masons of the World (irregular), ncd. Most Worshipful Lodge of Light (irregular), ncd. American Federation of Human Rights (mixed, irregular), http://www.co-masonry.org. Le Droit Humain American Federation (mixed), http://www.comasonic.org.

Utah: Grand Lodge of Utah Free and Accepted Masons, http://www.utahgrandlodge.org, email utahgs@email.com. (Prince Hall Masonry, established by Grand Lodge of Texas and Colorado.)

Vermont: Grand Lodge of Vermont Free and Accepted Masons, http://www.vtfreemasons.org/grandlodge.htm, email glsec@vtfreemasons.org. (No Prince Hall Masonry is known in the state.)

Virginia: Grand Lodge of Virginia Ancient Free and Accepted Masons, http://www.grandlodgeofvirginia.org, email grandlodge@rcn.com. Most Worshipful Prince Hall Grand Lodge of Virginia, Inc, http://www.mwphgl-va.org. Free and Accepted Masons of Demoncratic Republics (irregular), http://www.realtycom.net/gl.

Washington: Grand Lodge of Washington Free and Accepted Masons, http://www.freemason-wa.org, email grandsecretary@freemason-wa.org. Most Worshipful Prince Hall Grand Lodge Free and Accepted Masons Washington and Jurisdiction, http://www.mwphglwa.org. The Deputy Sovereign Grand Lodge of the Philippine Archipelago in America (irregular), ncd. American Federation of Human Rights (mixed, irregular), http://www.co-masonry.org. Le Droit Humain American Federation (mixed), http://www.comasonic.org.

West Virginia: Grand Lodge of West Virginia Ancient Free and Accepted Masons, http://www.wvmasons.org. Most Worshipful Prince Hall Grand Lodge of West Virginia Free and Accepted Masons, Inc., tel. +1 304 239 2731. American Federation of Human Rights (mixed, irregular), http://www.co-masonry.org. Le Droit Humain American Federation (mixed), http://www.comasonic.org.

Wisconsin: Grand Lodge of Wisconsin Free and Accepted Masons, http://www.wisc-freemasonry.org, email glo@wisc-freemasonry.org. Most Worshipful Prince Hall Grand Lodge Free and Accepted Masons of Wisconsin, Inc., http://www.wiprincehallgrandlodge.org. American Federation of Human Rights (mixed, irregular), http://www.co-masonry.org. Le Droit Humain American Federation (mixed), http://www.comasonic.org.

Wyoming: Grand Lodge of Wyoming Ancient Free and Accepted Masons, http://www.wyomingmasons.com, email grandsecretary@wyomingmasons.com. (Prince Hall Masonry, established by Grand Lodge of Colorado.)

Figures in italics indicate captions.

INDEX

AUTHOR ACKNOWLEDGEMENTS

Special thanks to Graham Pattenden for helping me get my facts straight, to Harry *and* Barbara Marment for years of friendship and support (among other reasons), and to the collected Brethren of Venture Adventure Lodge under the United Grand Lodge of England – a kinder, funnier, wiser and more generous group of men you will not find.

Tim Dedopulos is at dedopulos@gmail.com

PICTURE CREDITS

The publishers would like to thank the following sources for their kind permission to reproduce the pictures in this book.

AKG London: 20, 51, 52, /Elie Bernager: 29 right, /Erich Lessing: 61

Corbis Images: 24, 82, /Archivo Iconografico, S.A: 103, /Bettmann: 53, 62 top, 67, 101 left, 102, 110 left, /Bojan Brecelj: 62 bottom, /Bradley Smith: 115, /Christine Osborne: 100, /Gianni Giansanti/Sygma: 64, /Historical Picture Archive: 12, /Hulton Deutsch: 99, /Hulton-Deutsch Collection: 25, /Jean-Bernard Vernier/Sygma: 95, /Leonard de Selva: 68, /Stapleton Collection: 101 right, /Tatiana Markow/Sygma: 91 right, 93, /Ted Spiegel: 106/7, /Zen Icknow: 5 right, 104, 119

Fortean Picture Library: 49

Getty Images: /Jim Lina/Taxi: 96

Mary Evans Picture Library: 25, 34, 77 left, /T.Higham: 76, /W T Green: 58

Mirrorpix: /John Rush EDI: 118

Photos 12: /Hachedé: 4 right, 8, 26, 27, 31 right, 109, 112, 121 left, /Oasis: 9, /Oronoz: 69

Rex Features: /Tanguy Jockmans: 91 left

Steven John Koeppe: 117

The Bridgeman Art Library: / 'Freemasonry Instructing the People', 1875 (colour litho), Mercereau, Charles (1822–64)/Musee du Grand Orient de France, Paris, France, Archives Charmet: 4 mid, 84, / 'Table of Beliefs and Duties of a Freemason', second half nineteenth century (colour litho), French School, (nineteenth century)/Bibliotheque Nationale, Paris, France, Archives Charmet: 18, / 'The Constitutions of the Freemasons' by Dr James Anderson (c.1680–1739) published in London 1723 (engraving), English School, (eighteenth century)/Bibliotheque Nationale, Paris, France, Archives Charmet: 19, /Masonic Initiation Ceremony of a Lady Freemason, early nineteenth century (w/colour), French School, (nineteenth century)/Musée du Grand Orient de France, Paris, France, Archives Charmet: 21, /Masonic badge or jewel worn by members of the Grand Stewards Lodge after 1841, mid-nineteenth century (silver gilt and gold), English School, (nineteenth century)/ © Library and Museum of Freemasonry, London, UK, reproduced by permission of the Grand Lodge of England: 32, /Zerubbabel Showing a Plan of Jerusalem to Cyrus (oil on canvas), Loo, Jacob or Jacques van (c.1614–1670)/Musee des Beaux-Arts, Orleans, France, Giraudon: 39, /St

Helen (oil on panel), Meloni, Altobello (fl.1497–1517)/ © Ashmolean Museum, University of Oxford, UK: 41, /The Building of Noah's Ark, from the Nuremberg Chronicle by Hartmann Schedel (woodcut), German School, (sixteenth century)/ © Lambeth Palace Library, London, UK: 42, /Building the Temple of Solomon, illustration from the Raphael Bible (gouache over an etched base on paper), Italian School, (eighteenth century)/ Private Collection, © Bonhams, London, UK: 45, /Santa Trinita Altarpiece, detail of the grieving angels, c.1434 (tempera and gold on panel), Angelico, Fra (Guido di Pietro) (c.1387–1455)/Museo di San Marco dell'Angelico, Florence, Italy: 46, /Collar of the eighteenth degree of the Ancient and Accepted Rite (Roix Croix) (embroidered silk), English School, (twentieth century)/ © Library and Museum of Freemasonry, London, UK, reproduced by permission of the Grand Lodge of England: 48, /Ms 3 f.66v Moses on Mount Sinai; ten commandments on scroll; representation of the Tabernacle, / © Lambeth Palace Library, London, UK: 57, /Cott Nero E II pt2 fol.100v The Templars before Philippe IV (1268–1314) and Pope Clement V (c.1260–1320), from 'The Chronicles of France' (vellum), Boucicaut Master, (fl.1390–1430) (and workshop)/British Library, London, UK: 70, /Roy 20 C VII f.42v Arrest of the Templars, 1308, /British Library, London, UK: 71 left, /Roy 20 C VII f.44v Burning of the Templars, c.1308, /British Library, London, UK: 71 right, /Portrait of Valentine Andreae (1568–1643), copy of a German engraving illustrated in 'History of Magic', published late nineteenth century (litho), German School, (seventeenth century) (after)/Private Collection, The Stapleton Collection: 73, /Symbolic diagram of the Garden of Eden before the Fall of Man, c.1892 (coloured ink on paper), Burnett, Elizabeth (fl.1890s)/Private Collection: 75, /The Constitutions of Freemasonry by James Anderson, frontispiece, published by John Senex and John Hook, London, 1723 (engraving) (b/w photo), Pine, John (1690–1756) /Bibliotheque Nationale, Paris, France, Archives Charmet: 79, /Silver gilt Royal arch breast jewel and ribbon of pierced and engraved type, 1924 (silver),/Private Collection, © Bonhams, London, UK: 80, /The English masonic lodges, c.1730 (engraving) (b/w photo), French School, (eighteenth century)/Bibliotheque des Arts Decoratifs, Paris, France, Archives Charmet: 81, / 'A Masonic Anecdote', a description of the exposure of a fraud, 'Balsamo' at a lodge in London, 1786 (engraving), /British Museum, London, UK: 83, /Masonic Reception in France, second half eighteenth century (gouache on paper), French School, (eighteenth century)/Bibliotheque Nationale, Paris, France, Archives Charmet: 85, /Drafting the Declaration of Independence in 1776, 1859 (engraving) (b/w photo), Chappel, Alonzo (1828–87)/ © Atwater Kent Museum of Philadelphia: 86, /Boston Tea Party; the 'Boston Boys' throwing the taxed tea into the Charles River, 1773 (hand coloured print), Anonymous/ Private Collection: 87, /Portrait of John James Howell Coe, 1820s (oil on canvas), English School, (nineteenth century)/ © Library and Museum of Freemasonry, London, UK, Reproduced by permission of the Grand Lodge of England: 92

Topham Picturepoint: 31 left, 72 right, 94 right, 107, 121 right, /Charles Walker: 4 left, 28, 36, 43, 59, 72 left, 88, 94 left, /Chris Fitzgerald/The Image Works: 11, /English Heritage/HIP: 14, 22, /Fortean: 98, 113, /Fotomas: 29 left, /Karl Prouse: 110 right, /Roger-Viollet Collection: 5 mid, 111, 116, /UPP: 6, /UPPA: 17

Wellcome Trust Library, London: 37, 40, 54, 60, 74, 77 right, 79

Every effort has been made to acknowledge correctly and contact the source and/or copyright holder of each picture and Carlton Books Limited apologises for any unintentional errors or omissions which will be corrected in future editions of this book.